THE NECESSITY OF CHOICE

THE NECESSITY OF CHOICE

Nineteenth-Century Political Thought

Louis Hartz

Edited, compiled, and prepared by
Paul Roazen

With a Preface by
Benjamin Barber

Transaction Publishers
New Brunswick (U.S.A.) and London (U.K.)

Library of Congress Catalog Number: 89-28039
ISBN: 0-88738-326-2
Printed in the United States of America

Library of Congress Cataloging-in-Publication Data

Hartz, Louis, 1919–1986.
    The necessity of choice : Nineteenth-Century political thought /
by Louis Hartz with an introduction and edited by Paul Roazen.
        p.   cm.
    Includes bibliographical references.
    ISBN 0-88738-326-2
    1. Political science—History—19th century.   I. Roazen, Paul,
1936–   . II. Title.
JA83.H28   1990
320.5′09′034—dc20   89–28039
                                                                                         CIP

Contents

Foreword

On January 20, 1986, Louis Hartz, former professor of government at Harvard University, died in Istanbul, Turkey. Despite a career abbreviated by illness (which compelled him to retire in 1974), Hartz had an enormous impact on both American political theory and debates about the nature and consequences of the American experience in his three decades of teaching and research in Cambridge.

At Harvard, he was a teacher of such extraordinary talent and energy and brought with him to the classroom a lecture style so charismatic and enduring that students could find themselves initially too overwhelmed to take very much in. I remember with pleasure Hart's wry if absent-minded blackboard doodlings that were meant to symbolize some subtle point in Benjamin Contant's liberalism or Frederick Jackson Turner's frontier thesis but which seemed finally only to capture the engagingly anarchic vivacity of his fast-moving mind.

Nor was he just a man for the classroom or a scholarly denizen of Widener library's well-furnished stacks. He felt the world deeply, and engaged it no less than its literary surrogates in his work. His books had so powerful an impact in part because one sensed their commitment to and engagement in the real world. After his illness made it impossible for him to teach and difficult for him to do archival research, he took to traveling—traversing random international roads in a disquieting quest for the meaning of world history. He was at work on a manuscript aimed at explaining East and West in terms of a great historical synthesis when he died. The project was of Spencerian ambitions and was clearly beyond the powers left him by his uncertain health, but

that he aspired to it suggests something of the nature of his
intellectual fortitude in the face of momentous difficulties.

Hartz admired the French liberals of the early nineteenth century—Constant, Comte, and above all Tocqueville—and, like
Tocqueville, he believed one had to see something of the world to
understand any of it. When in the early 1960s I hesitantly proposed to him that I spend some time in Switzerland to research a
dissertation on the Swiss understanding of political liberty—he
had originally consented to direct a dissertation that had been
conceived in purely philosophical terms—he responded without
an instant's doubt: "Yes, yes, yes, of course, you must go—go to
the Alps, stay, live there, get a feel for the Grisons, you can write
me from time to time, but get over there until you have captured
what you see on paper."

His writing demonstrated that he practiced what he preached.
His *The Liberal Tradition in America,* published in 1955 and the
winner in 1956 of the Woodrow Wilson Prize of the American
Political Science Association, offered a powerful explanation for
the dominion of Lockean consensualism in America, and set the
parameters for a historical and philosophical debate that was also
profoundly political and that in subsequent years was to be joined
by such eminent historians as Bernard Bailyn, J. G. A. Pocock,
and John Diggins—thoughtful commentators who debated the
nature of the American founding and its impact on how we see
ourselves as a nation in terms of problems set by Hartz. Hartz
used Tocqueville's observation that the Americans had "arrived at
a state of democracy without having to endure a democratic
revolution" as the starting place for an argument focused on the
absence of a feudal tradition in the new world, and how that
absence explained the prevalence of a form of centralist consensualism that would have been unthinkable in the old world. America's exceptionalist experience endowed it with a certain immunity
to radicalism in general and socialism in particular, and made it a
poor candidate for socioeconomic explanations of the kind that
flourished in the setting of postfeudal European ideology. A
people born into equality, Hartz suggested, might perceive in
peoples who were compelled to win their equality by will and
revolution only a profound mystery. What distinguished the
American from the European ideology was what was missing in

America: a heritage of feudalism. That absent heritage rendered the ideological rhetoric of both feudalism and socialism, class conflict and class hegemony, irrelevant to America. Locke's American meaning was given less by the empty places (Locke's *vacuis locis*) of the new world's vast territory than by the empty pages of the new world's missing history.

In the 1960s, Bernard Bailyn responded to Hartz by arguing that English dissent ideology had played a more prominent role in the American founding than Hartz's preoccupation with the absence of feudalism could acknowledge. In the 1970s, J. G. A. Pocock and other students of the Atlantic Republican tradition offered a portrait of America in which classical republican virtue played a larger role than either Lockean consensualism or dissent philosophy. Most recently, John Diggins has refocused attention on Hartz by suggesting that a rather Calvinist version of Locke played a crucial role in the constitutional founding if not in the revolution, and that this splintered Lockean inheritance, encompassing both interest and religious passion, can be traced down to Lincoln where, unhappily for America, it begins to disappear. The debate today has come full circle then, no longer confined to Lockean consensualism, but its terms still largely defined by Hartz's brilliant portrait of the liberal tradition.

Yet what is perhaps most important about Hartz is not the particular conclusions his analysis led to about the American experience, but his insistence on a comparative method that looked at national experiences in terms of comparative historical genealogy. As the comparison of the American ideology with its European progenitors revealed what was missing in America—the feudal experience—so Hartz supposed that an examination of other "new " societies founded in the shadow of colonial patrimonies might reveal certain secrets of their national heritages. Thus, in a book Hartz edited in 1964 called *The Founding of New Societies,* he and several colleagues subjected Latin America, Canada, South Africa, and Australia, as well as the United States, to the test of a comparison with the European cultures that spawned them. There the specific thesis about America offered in *The Liberal Tradition in America* was transformed into a general hypothesis about new societies:

When a part of a European nation is detached from the whole of it, and hurled outward onto new soil, it loses the stimulus toward change that the whole provides. It lapses into a kind of immobility . . . the fragments reflect every phase of European revolution, but they evince alike the immobilities of fragmentation . . . their escape has turned out to be an illusion, and they are forced now to transcend the conservatism to which it gave birth.

From his early book on economics and democracy in Pennsylvania (*Economic Policy and Democratic Thought: Pennsylvania, 1776–1860*) Hartz had concerned himself with the interpenetration of old and new cultures, of colonial nations and their elusive offspring, hoping thereby to illuminate and strengthen the democratic experience. In that final unfinished, and probably unfinishable, manuscript he was working on sporadically in the years before his death, Hartz clearly hoped to achieve a synthesis of world history. In this synthesis Europe with its principles of rational technology and domination, and the non-Western world with its more pliant intuitive cultures and its saving devotion to inner values, were to be reconciled. Unlike those many Western observers who have foreseen the inevitable victory of the West (for better or, as the critics often believe, for worse), he envisioned an eventual convergence of the two forms of culture—although not before a tremendous "battle fought out in a distant hour on the streets of the world city [that] cannot be described." And not before all humankind was brought to experience "the terror of the clashing elements of striving and surrender that lie at the heart of life."

Hartz's terminal struggles with the meaning of the world were clearly personal as well as professional and involved him in a long battle for clarity that he could only hope to half-win. The battle had to have been painful for him in the extreme, and those of us who were his beneficiaries as students and citizens and who learned from him the passion that is political theory can only feel grateful that he has now been relieved of its weight. For "the terror of the clashing elements of striving and surrender that lie at the heart of life" is no mere historical metaphor, but, as Louis Hartz knew, and the honest and the brave among us must slowly learn, is the reality and the essence of human life in the twentieth century.

BENJAMIN R. BARBER

Introduction

Paul Roazen

Louis Hartz's Teaching

Louis Hartz was the greatest teacher I ever had, and his death at the age of 66 in early 1986 has reminded me of the need to try to recapture his contribution and transmit it to others. He once was asked to write a short piece on teaching, and the essence of his brief argument was that a scholar performs his educational functions best as he offers himself to students as an example of how to proceed. On the lecture platform and in small classes he was a dazzlingly brilliant political theorist at work. By his own standard he succeeded as a teacher, certainly with me, and yet in the end he seemed to fail spectacularly. Since he retired from Harvard in 1974, under unusual and tragic circumstances, by now he has disappeared from the imaginations of a whole new generation of intellectuals.

I remember with absolute clarity the first time I laid eyes on his great book, *The Liberal Tradition in America: An Interpretation of American Political Thought Since the Revolution*.[1] It not only went on to win the highest professional awards a political scientist could hope for, but its continued survival in the general culture ensures the standing and reputation he now has. During the spring of 1955, in my freshman year at Harvard, I spotted a stack of the new book displayed in a corner of the front window of the Harvard Coop. Then it had become fashionable to talk about the "new Conservatism," a movement of thought advocated by a set of writers distinctly different from our own so-called neoconservatives. Walter Lippmann's *The Public Philosophy* had come out that term and was the source of

1

much talk about the limits on the public's rationality; in rebuttal some writers challenged Lippmann's pessimistic assessment of democracy with their own passionate defenses of the traditional values of American progressivism. Other controversial books were then appearing from the Right by such different writers as Russell Kirk, Peter Viereck, and Clinton Rossiter; so it was not surprising that my section man in the introductory course in government offered one essay, among other alternatives, on conservatism.

I bought Hartz's book to help my term-paper writing. But to my surprise and mild irritation I found that I could not understand it. I do not think I can have tried to read more than a few pages, but it was clearly a hopeless endeavor for the practical purposes I had in mind. That summer I was at loose ends, and decided to audit a couple of lecture courses at Harvard Summer School. One was on the modern novel, which I went to for the sake of my general education, and the other was a course of Hartz's entitled American and British Political Thought, which I attended out of curiosity and frustration over my inability to make sense of *The Liberal Tradition in America*.

Over the summer months I read a number of important long novels, but it was Hartz's lectures that captured my imagination and influenced the future course of my work. I had never heard anyone like Hartz; his small class was a whirl of ideas, all of which fit into a larger structure. Political theory had already been taught to me in terms of writers and their works, but Hartz was concerned with issues, and he was as challenging in terms of the demanding nature of the sequence of his thought as he was appealing in his willingness to offer resolutions to the dilemmas he posed.

I had already read a few of the books on the reading list, and I poked about in some of the assignments, but it was clear that the excitement in this series of classes had nothing to do with the texts that supposedly were required reading. If you took or audited all of Hartz's classes, as I eventually did, you began to see a pattern in his assigning a book in one course only to discuss it in another. It was not a matter of professorial absentmindedness, but I suspected that he considered it an insult to our intelligence simply to go over something in class that we could read on our own.

As I look over my lecture notes from that first course of his, I am struck by how little attention he paid to American political thought, and he also dealt only a bit with British political theorists. In my notes I find that he remarked at the outset of the course that in America the significant political thinking took place in the pre-Civil War South. But after having made that striking point he immediately launched into a planned discussion of the French and American Revolutions and eighteenth-century ideals; he was more concerned with continental thought than with any American writers. Hartz went on to talk about nineteenth-century liberal thought, and he did touch on some British thinkers. But throughout the course he was more preoccupied with France, and also with socialism, than with anything explicitly to do with the incomprehensible book that had brought me to his class in the first place.

I do not recall even noticing that American subjects were being slighted. In hindsight, Hartz might have been trying to get away from the book of his that had just appeared. It turned out that he had been arguing its thesis for several years, and his classes were the audience before whom he hammered together the approach in *The Liberal Tradition in America*. Hartz sent off so many fireworks that summer that I did not notice or care whether he had been unfair to any one particular writer or period, or even if he had, in this course at any rate, ignored almost all American political thinkers.

His genuine achievement was to explore, in a thoroughly organized set of lectures, the social setting of political philosophers and to describe in a comparative way the kinds of characteristic differences between political theory in Europe and America. In his first lecture, for example, he maintained that the eighteenth-century background to the French and American revolutions had been wholly different. In France there was an immensely complicated social system, torn by internal divisions provoked by the rising middle class challenging a decaying agrarian feudal system. Successive kings had been using their bureaucrats to encroach on the power of the nobles, and therefore unwittingly had been hostile to "the very system of society of which they themselves were the traditional apex." Hartz loved to instruct by means of paradoxes.

England, he argued, had its own class antagonisms. As in France, independent craftsmen were being undermined by the spread of merchant capitalism. However, the British aristocracy had a special capacity for absorbing the wealthy bourgeoisie, and therefore the animosities toward a privileged but increasingly functionless nobility that France saw were lessened in England.

In contrast to both France and Britain, America lacked a feudal heritage. No aristocratic class existed to confront the merchants, nor any guild organizations to object to the creation of permanent laborers. The American scene lacked the frustration and hostility that marked the French case, and to a lesser degree the English.

Revolution, Hartz believed, was not produced by misery but by the pressure of a new system on an old one.[2] But in America no revolution comparable to the great European conflicts had taken place. The Americans revolted against imperial restrictions; they had been engaged in colonial rather than social struggles. Social changes did take place in America after 1776; vestiges of feudalism like primogeniture were abolished, and Tory estates were broken up. But what was of marginal importance in America became central in France's struggles against the ancien régime. And conflicts within the democratic forces who seized control in America at the end of the eighteenth century would be in no way similar to the European situation.

Hartz's second lecture followed conceptually from the first. In France the impact of an emerging middle class against a weakened feudal structure produced the spark of the Enlightenment and revolution. Hartz pursued the role of the intellectual in France in helping to break down the accepted norms of the traditional social mythology. The philosophes exploited grievances that were implicit in the existing social tensions. The weak French censorship encouraged critical opinion and helped whet the appetite for challenge.

The ancien régime, Hartz believed, had not been unified in imposing its repressions. In attacking the old system, the social agitators could ally with the monarchy. Voltaire, among others, thought that salvation lay with enlightened despotism. At the same time the monarchy protected the philosophes, who attacked the power of the Church. The nobility, which sometimes looked with favor on the philosophes, did not see the danger of its being undermined by corrosive social speculation. The philosophes flourished because of the internal divisions in the ancien régime.

In America the opposition came not from the generalities of the philosophes but from the specific grievances of practical men. The colonial legislatures took the lead, and the politicians were only forced by circumstances to become theorists. The Americans could be more sober and responsible as they proposed new adjustments. In the absence of a feudal order, people like Sam Adams or James Otis could act on behalf of an already established responsible government. In America the clergy, instead of being a source of corruption and intolerance, would lead the struggle for change in a situation that was not socially revolutionary.

Those first two lectures Hartz gave serve now, as they did then, to introduce the nature of his work; he gave another stimulating twenty-three before the summer course was over. Individual insights that he advanced had been anticipated before by others. But no one had put them together as he had, with the same purposes in mind. He went on to make Jean-Jacques Rousseau a leading figure in the course, but he also lectured on the physiocrats, Jeremy Bentham, John Stuart Mill, and Karl Marx. One lecture was on why England did not have a revolution; another touched on the nature of human freedom, and he worked all this into the fate of nationalism in Italy and Germany.

If, as Hartz believed, philosophizing exists only where there is fundamental social conflict, it is no wonder that American political thought, compared to what happened in Europe, never succeeded in getting off the ground. My notes from that course do not indicate that he ever once returned to his point about the creativity that took place in the antebellum American South. According to Hartz the issues in American history had lacked the basic character of European conflicts. And he thought that the American experience was unique in the context of the political principles common to Western Europe.

By the end of that summer's course I had no trouble tackling *The Liberal Tradition in America*. Hartz's work was so much the topic of professional conversation that I explicated his book in writing a paper the next year on "The Liberal Society Analysis" for my sophomore tutorial. I suppose it was because of a kind of missionary spirit that I had acquired that I did not then mention a blunder Hartz had made in the epigraph to his book. He had quoted Alexis de Tocqueville as having written in *Democracy in America*: "The great advantage of the American is that he has arrived at a state of democracy without having to endure a democratic revolution; and that he is born free without having to become so." However, de Tocqueville had said "born equal," not born free, and an errata slip appeared in fresh copies of that first printing. Only the narrow-minded took Hartz's mistake too seriously; his thesis was arresting enough to capture and hold attention.

Although I did not realize it at the time, the words "liberal" and "liberalism" had only recently appeared in the American political vocabulary. They entered the language of American politics in the early years of Franklin Roosevelt's administration, and afterwards they stood for the viewpoint of the New Deal. It was innovative of Hartz at the outset of the 1950s, in his first journal articles on the subject, to try to make liberalism the key to American political thought. At the same time the tenor of Hartz's approach had its echos in other writings of that time. David Riesman's *The Lonely Crowd*[3] and his essays collected in *Individualism Reconsidered*[4] were written in a spirit akin to Hartz's; Lionel Trilling's *The Liberal Imagination*[5] was also a like-minded work with implications for social and political thought.

Essentially Hartz was proposing a new, full-scale theory about the course of American history. Part I of the book, which was also the first chapter, was titled "Feudalism and the American Experience," and Hartz relentlessly explored the implications of his thesis. If America had essentially been a liberal society from the outset, and had had no need for a revolution on a European scale, then that explained why America also had lacked a Reaction and the tradition of genuine conservatism that was so characteristically a part of European political thought. The issue of the nature of conservatism may have been what brought me to Hartz's book, but his theory went far beyond that one matter.

Hartz used America's relative lack of class conflict to explain socialism's weakness as well. While Marx had seen his doctrines as a by-product of industrialization, Hartz thought that socialism was "largely an ideological phenomenon, arising out of the principles of class and the revolutionary liberal revolt against them which the old European order inspired."[6] Hartz was, like at the time Perry Miller in literature and Talcott Parsons in sociology, emphasizing the powerful historical role of the life of the mind. Ideas had consequences and were not just reflexive of social circumstances. Hartz's liberal society thesis meant that it was understandable why Americans could have been satisfied with a system of checks and balances, federalism, and separation of powers, which could only have worked in the context of a basically unified society. For in America the state had never been charged with the same purposes of reform that European leftists like Bentham and Voltaire had intended for it.

Although *The Liberal Tradition in America* might appear to reflect the supposed complacency of the 1950s, in fact the whole book represented a challenge to American thinking. He was trying to expose a fixed, dogmatic liberalism in American life. It was, he held, only because of the nature of the American liberal consensus that so much attention could be paid to technique rather than first principles. The unique position of the Supreme Court in America and "the cult of constitution worship"[7] meant that issues that in other countries might be morally debated were in America consigned to lawyers and adjudication. Law "flourished on the corpse of philosophy in America, for the settlement of the ultimate moral question is the end of speculation upon it."[8] The moral unanimity of liberal American society meant that too much in America had gone irrationally unchallenged.

Hartz used the name of John Locke to symbolize the kind of liberalism characteristic of America: consent was the ultimate basis for political obligation; political communities arose out of the rational agreement of its individual members; and individual liberties, including importantly property rights, were the ultimate purposes for which the legitimate community existed. Hartz was not citing Locke for purposes of technical philosophical analysis, nor was Hartz making a historical argument about how frequently the colonists read Locke, or cited him. Hartz had little interest in the study of political ideas as a scholastic exercise but rather wanted to use Locke as a symbol for a brand of political thought that could illuminate political reality.

Although Hartz's interpretation came to be associated with a so-called consensus school of American history, his starting point was political theory, and he did not have in mind a naïve celebration of the American way of life. He was alarmed by the "deep and unwritten tyrannical compulsion" contained in the unanimity of American liberalism.[9] Hartz thought that Lockianism inherently contained within itself an individualistic spirit that transcended conformism, and he appealed for encouragement to the examples of Oliver Wendell Holmes, Jr., Learned Hand, Louis Brandeis, Franklin D. Roosevelt, and Adlai Stevenson. But he hoped that the perspective that would enable America to overcome its provincialism might arise from the new significance for the country of world politics. He wondered whether American liberalism could "acquire through external experience that sense of relativity, that spark of philosophy which European liberalism acquired through an internal experience of social diversity and social conflict."[10]

Hartz was not trying, as it has been so often alleged of him, to emphasize solidarity in order to minimize the significance of conflict in American history or to downgrade the importance of the struggles that had taken place. He was instead trying to describe the ideological circumference in which conflicts in America had occurred. The American Right had its parallels in the European tradition of large-propertied liberalism; and the American Left could best be understood in connection with the European petit bourgeois tradition. Jefferson had once maintained that "we are all republicans—we are all federalists."[11] By putting American history in the context of a comparative historical analysis Hartz thought that one could begin to see the nature of specifically American problems.

Hartz conceded that what he was proposing was a single factor analysis: "the absence of feudalism and the presence of the liberal idea."[12] In the teeth of the fashionability of multi-causality in social science Hartz wanted to isolate what he regarded as a single historical variable and to study it by consistently comparing historical experiences in America with those in Europe.

In contrast to other theories of American history, such as Frederick Jackson Turner's emphasis on the significance of the frontier, Hartz could point out that many countries had had their frontiers without the result being anything like liberal democracy. But in general Hartz's approach did not arise to challenge Turner's historiography or that of the other Progressive historians. Hartz did think that Charles Beard's view of class conflict, like Arthur Bentley's group analysis, took for granted the context in which social struggles took place. American studies have been, Hartz thought, promoted by nationalist forces that were blind to a comparative perspective.[13] While progressive historians saw pendulum-like swings recurring throughout the American past, he thought his own outlook was less complacently confident that political virtue would eventually triumph.

Hartz picked four main periods in American history to illustrate the power of his liberal society analysis: the American Revolution, Jacksonianism, the South before the Civil War, and the epoch symbolized by the writings of Horatio Alger. He ended with a discussion of the significance of the New Deal and America's world involvement. Hartz's book was over-cooked and not easy to read since he took for granted that his readers were well versed in European and American history. He littered his text with the names of thinkers who might be familiar to students of intellectual history, but who were bound to sound unusual in an interpretive work about American political thought.

It commonly has been thought that the most momentous part of Hartz's book was the material about the revolutionary period. There is little doubt that his categories have permanently affected the way historians treat that phase. The books that were written by the Founding Fathers, and the arguments that they advanced both against the British as well as in behalf of the new Constitution, represent a permanent addition to Western thought. Hartz's interpretive approach was the more powerful when it was addressed to works in intellectual history.

I think that the most novel chapter in the book was the one called "The Reactionary Enlightenment," in which he resurrected George Fitzhugh as a political theorist. A few years later, when C. Vann Woodward wrote an introduction to a reprinted edition of one of Fitzhugh's books, Woodward immediately acknowledged his indebtedness to Hartz's previous work.[14] But while Woodward was balanced and thorough, placing Fitzhugh in his historical setting, it had been Hartz's striking chapter that changed people's minds.

Fitzhugh was a neglected writer from a forgotten school of thought until Hartz called attention to him. Hartz was fascinated by Fitzhugh's challenge to the American liberal unity. Fitzhugh had not only defended slavery but had done so within terms outside a liberal framework. Fitzhugh saw the merits of hierarchy, restraint, and order and at the same time assailed the North for embodying a worse form of tyranny than anything the South practiced. The doctrine of laissez-faire was to Fitzhugh a version of unmitigated selfishness, and led to "wage slavery."[15] Fitzhugh was, for Hartz, a critic of Northern capitalist values, and not just a defender of the old South. Like European conservative thinkers, Fitzhugh saw the hypocrisy behind the Northern commitment to freedom. Genuine liberty requires a social basis for support, while to Fitzhugh the freedom of the Northern working man was a fiction. As this argument was re-created by Hartz, Fitzhugh appeared as a lonely seer able to break through the conventional thinking of American culture.

At the same time there was something half-cracked about Fitzhugh, and Hartz thought that Fitzhugh's perverse social task meant that one could hardly blame him for ultimately having broken down. For what kind of conservative could Fitzhugh be, living in a section of the country that honored Thomas Jefferson so centrally among its forefathers? While Fitzhugh could assail the encroachments of the North, he did not seem able to acknowledge the degree to which the South was part of a tradition of liberalism. William Lloyd Garrison once refused to answer Fitzhugh's attack, saying: "argument is demanded—to prove what?"[16] It seemed self-evident to Garrison that Fitzhugh's charges were historically beside the point, and that was for Hartz a sure sign that Garrison, and not Fitzhugh, was a representative man. Fitzhugh was fascinating precisely because the problem of slavery drove him beyond the insights typical of liberalism, but at the time his iconoclasm appeared irrelevant to the nation's experience.

Hartz's own book did not suffer the immediate fate of Fitzhugh's writings. *The Liberal Tradition in America* was widely recognized as a landmark in the understanding of American political thinking. Arthur Schlesinger, Jr. was one of the earliest who restated Hartz's argument in a more accessible form, even though Schlesinger suspected that Hartz's approach minimized an important diversity in American thinking. Another article in the *Partisan Review* presented Hartz's thesis for its special audience; and one symposium drew journal articles by intellectual historians reconsidering *The Liberal Tradition in America*. Richard Hofstadter had immediately admired Hartz's contribution; in 1968 he wrote some pages about Hartz's work in relation to Progressive historiography: "the influence of Hartz's book reflects the importance, indeed the classic centrality, of his ideas."[17] Garry Wills, in his *Nixon Agonistes* (1970), paused to spell out the direction of Hartz's thought. As early as the late 1950s, when it was first apparent that a "consensus" school of thought was threatening to homogenize the American past, the historian John Higham singled out Hartz's book as "perhaps the most outstanding of the new interpretive books." Yet while Higham worried about the dangers of a "cult" of consensus, he recognized that Hartz's "own sympathies lay with dissent and diversity."[18]

Curiously enough the most savage onslaught on Hartz had come from Daniel J. Boorstin, the former librarian of Congress but then a professor at the University of Chicago. Boorstin's own *The Genius of American Politics* (1953) had generously acknowledged the power of Hartz's insights. "Parts of this volume," Boorstin wrote in a review for *Commentary,* "have already appeared as brief essays in learned journals, and in that form seemed brilliant. But," Boorstin went on, "this is not the work we had hoped for from Mr. Hartz." Boorstin's own thesis about the absence of political theory in America has often been compared to Hartz's, and in later years Boorstin amplified his interest in social history by means of his three-volume *The Americans*. But Boorstin, an ex-Marxist, then saw Hartz as a prisoner of European comparisons. "He seems unable to describe what is characteristically American except by enumerating the several peculiarly European phenomena which have happened to be absent from American history." Boorstin's own writing is simple and direct—which later helped lead to best-sellerdom—so he was affronted by Hartz's style: "Mr. Hartz's obviously lively mind expresses itself not in new insights but in the translation of cliché into paradox." Boorstin objected to Hartz's stylistic obscurities, and also to Hartz's "prodigious bookishness"; he alleged that Hartz had "a weakness for mistaking books for life," and to him, therefore, *The Liberal Tradition in America* was "a monument of hyper-intellectualism."[19]

Marvin Meyers, also then of the University of Chicago, objected to Boorstin's attack: "I think he mistook the abundant signs of Professor Hartz's learning for his thesis and method. To me the remarkable feature of this book on political thought is the regular substitution of nonintellectual categories for ideas. It is basically, I think, a study of the *un*conscious mind of America, conditioned by a peculiar historical and social experience."[20] Despite Boorstin's attack from a conservative direction, Hartz's name and that of Boorstin were to remain permanently linked as part of a distinctive approach to American history. Yet Boorstin's judgment of Hartz's book shows how at odds with the new conservatism Hartz really was.

Hartz's book was indeed complicated, and I have reread it more times than any other contemporary text. Each time I have gone through *The Liberal Tradition in America* I have found insights that are new to me as his argument freshly illuminated writers with whom I had become more familiar.

When I first successfully read it through, however, it simply made me want to take more courses by Hartz. In my junior year at Harvard I enrolled in a graduate course on Nineteenth-Century Political Thought. It was primarily about European thinkers, and it remains the greatest series of lectures I have ever heard. My huge stack of notes makes me remember how exhilarated rather than exhausted I was by note-taking at the time. Hartz's passionate lecturing highlighted what he saw as the key issues in modern political theory: what is the good society, and how can the state help realize it? Hartz's own interests were to shift so radically in the direction of comparative history that he never published a line from the greatest of his courses. (In the second part of this Introduction I will examine the circumstances of the text of *The Necessity of Choice: Nineteenth-Century Political Thought.*)

He did, however, once publish an article drawn from a popular undergraduate course called Democratic Theory and Its Critics, which I audited before I graduated.[21] Hartz had been one of the post-World War II proponents of general education at Harvard, and while that generation of scholars who believed in the creation of the program have now all passed from the teaching scene, and the general education courses have been replaced by a different curriculum, a version of the same course is still being taught at Harvard. In the 1950s the identical course was being given by students of Hartz all across the country. It was typical of Hartz's approach that although political theory was the most traditional field in political science, his own courses were unique and identifiably his own.

In Democratic Theory and Its Critics he outlined the classical defense of liberalism as articulated by Locke, Bentham, and Rousseau, and then he showed how it fared in the face of twentieth-century challenges. Hartz was proposing to try to preserve the ideals of democracy in the face of fresh insights on the part of modern thinkers.

He presented the ideas of the English guild socialists and the American pluralists; he taught Freud and elitist theorists; and he articulated the challenge of socialist ideology. His objective was to reconstruct liberalism in the light of these twentieth-century schools of thought. Students came away with an understanding of what some of the key problems associated with democratic theory might be.

By the time I knew him Hartz was moving away from a concern with the mainstream of political thought and attempt-

ing to understand comparative history as a whole. He had a
Toynbeean tendency, and evidently aspired to understand all
of world history. My own inclinations were more prosaic, and
although I once wrote a graduate paper for him comparing the
reception of Freud's ideas in America and Britain, a synthetic
approach to world history was not my cup of tea.

I did audit a graduate course Hartz taught on American
historiography and certainly made note of the 1964 appearance
of his *The Founding of New Societies*.[22] With the help of four
distinguished collaborators Hartz had extended his insight into
American history to help understand the central strands in the
experiences of Latin America, South Africa, Canada, and Australia. For each of these histories there would now be a
"Hartzian" interpretation.[23]

My own work was then on the mundane issues of Ph.D. thesis
writing. I chose Hartz as my supervisor, which in that department at Harvard meant that if he approved my work that was
essentially all the backing I would need. I remember proposing
to write on the ideas of Thomas Hobbes but hesitated, telling
Hartz that I might not be ready to take on such an immense
figure as Hobbes. "If not now," he said to me, "when?" Hartz
has always remained for me a model of intellectual daring and
integrity.

When it came to my actual thesis on "Freud and Political
Theory," Hartz remained personally distant and yet in some
basic way thoroughly supportive. I was his head course assistant
in his Democratic Theory and Its Critics, and we chatted on
informal occasions. He once said to me that he regretted
neglecting the role of race in his *The Liberal Tradition in America*. When a draft of my thesis was finished, we had lunch once
to discuss it, and he challenged me so about what my work had
added up to that the luncheon successfully forced me to write a
new conclusion to the dissertation.

After earning my Ph.D. in 1965 I was able to stay on to teach
in the government department. I will never forget the despair I
felt about myself, when I first began lecturing, after I once
again heard him perform in class. My only consolation was that
there was no necessary reason that I had to proceed like him,
although in my heart I knew my own work could be more

structured. Before giving his own lectures I had seen him sitting alone in an isolated coffee shop totally concentrated on his lecture notes.

By the late 1960s Hartz was already more than a little out of it in terms of departmental politics. I recall one of my other teachers remarking that unfortunately, when it came to Hartz's students, he thought that every goose he had was a swan. But I believe that at that time Hartz still had some exceptionally promising pupils. They did not go to Hartz, as some students went to others, for the sake of future patronage; he never had his eye on possible job openings. He discouraged me from continuing as his head course assistant, since at that stage of my career Hartz thought it would be demeaning for both of us. He was unlike some university potentates who exploited young faculty members. At that time there were plenty who believed he was the best in the field.

Before I left Harvard in 1971 there were events, personal as well as political, that overshadowed the Hartz I had known. I now had my own books to think about writing, and the world of Southeast Asia gradually overwhelmed former allegiances in the university community. I knew that Hartz was no longer speaking to some of his old friends in the government department. He was more remote than ever from daily events, although during at least one departmental meeting, in a university crisis, he was as frighteningly articulate and persuasive as ever.

Hartz took me to an elegant dinner in the fall of 1971, and then it so happened that I never saw him again. He spoke with enthusiasm about how hard he had been working, and yet it was obvious to me that realistically nothing special was coming out of it. He had already separated from his wife, whom I had known a bit socially. Then two years later, when I was securely settled in Canada, I heard secondhand awful stories about the end of his career at Harvard. He evidently had had some sort of a paranoid breakdown; he had heard meaningful noises if not voices, would not take a sick leave, and finally retired on a measly sum. His name disappeared from the departmental roster. Fortunately I had not had to witness what happened.

Hartz dropped everyone that I know of with whom he had

once been friendly. Through a friend in the government department I heard that Hartz had been in India for a time, then in London, and later back in New York City. He was reported to be as well-dressed as ever. He even produced a manuscript for a book, which when I saw it seemed unpublishable, but Hartz had it privately printed abroad.[24] I wrote Hartz a letter once, by means of a circuitous route that had been recommended to me, about my desire to publish his lectures on nineteenth-century political thought; I was not surprised that I never received any answer.

The year before Hartz died, John P. Diggins published *The Lost Soul of American Politics,* a book in which Hartz's *The Liberal Tradition in America* plays a central role.[25] Diggins was never Hartz's pupil, but Hartz's work was still so current that Diggins could absorb the ideas from Hartz's writing for the sake of criticizing more recent interpreters of America. When Diggins's book was reviewed in the Sunday *New York Times,* Hartz was described as "the great Harvard theorist." The reviewer, although I had not realized it at the time, had also been a student of Hartz.

Teaching involves both illusion and reality, and therefore when it comes to being self-critical about the impact Hartz had on me I am unsure. There is no doubt that he went completely off-the-rails. Was Hartz's fate worse or just as bad as Perry Miller's drinking himself to death, openly sipping from a flask before going inside a building to deliver a lecture? If I analyze the odd position Hartz staked out for himself within a political science moving in an entirely different direction from his own, toward policy studies or behavioralism but not intellectual history, a breakdown—as with Fitzhugh—might seem almost rational.

And yet it strikes me as humanly memorable how, when I take up those lecture notes I wrote down as an undergraduate, the striking figure Hartz was comes rushing back. Thirty years later I can testify to the unforgettable brilliance of his teaching. The *New York Times* is in some sense the Vatican of our intellectual life; I do not know how their obituary staff got on to the significance of Hartz's death (in Istanbul), but their writer, David Margolick, did a fine job. "In more than three decades at

Harvard, Mr. Hartz lectured to thousands of undergraduates." Lots of others have done as much, but then Margolick's obituary included a sentence that sums up what I have tried to say, too: "A small, energetic man who moved perpetually, and spoke in rapid-fire fashion, he infused his students with his passion for ideas."[26] Louis Hartz has been gone for a long time now, which means that it is high time his teaching was commemorated.

The Place of *The Necessity of Choice: Nineteenth-Century Political Thought*

When I last saw Hartz, during dinner in the fall of 1971, I did raise the issue of my wanting eventually to publish my notes of his lectures from that memorable course of his. By then his real consuming interests had shifted away from the subject. I could tell he was both pleased and flattered by my suggestion, but at the moment I had plenty of other projects at hand, and it never dawned on me that this might be the last time I would see him. Since he did seem to like my idea, I am proceeding as if I had gotten his approval.

Since his death it has proved impossible to track down Hartz's own lecture notes. One has to assume, I am afraid, that they are now never likely to turn up. As I recall it, when I took the graduate course myself in the fall of 1956 he had typed lecture notes at hand, which on occasion cracked with age as he worked from them in class. I was a junior in the government department at Harvard at the time, and doubtless my own note-taking would have been less obsessively thorough if I had encountered the course at a more mature stage in my own development. In the summer of 1966 I assisted Hartz in giving the course at Harvard's Summer School, but I had no reason to think that the approach Hartz took then had altered in any way.

In the course of my deliberating on making a book out of my lecture notes, I had occasion to ask others either to check my narrative by reading it through or else to supply me with their version of the lectures in the form of their own notes. Professor Michael P. Rogin of the Department of Political Science at the University of California, Berkeley, took the course the same term I did, and he was the first to have gone through one of my early drafts with his painstaking conscientiousness; he checked his own notes for corrections to suggest. Professor Alan Ritter, also Hartz's student and now at the University of Connecticut Law School, read that early draft for me too, making his own comments and improvements. I also want to thank Professor Asher Horowitz of the Department of Political Science at York University in Toronto for having read through the whole text; although he was never a pupil of Hartz, I relied on his general good sense and competency in the more recent scholarly literature in the field.

Professor Gad Horowitz of the Department of Political Science at the University of Toronto, who has so notably contributed to a Hartzian interpretation of Canada, cooperatively loaned me his own lecture notes. And I am particularly grateful for the many benefits I derived from studying the notes taken down by Professor Benjamin R. Barber of the Department of Politics at Rutgers University; at certain points they proved critical in my construction of the final text.

But the biggest single textual debt I owe is to Professor Herbert J. Spiro of the Freie Universität Berlin; he took the course while he was, like myself, an undergraduate, but it was in the spring of 1949, some long years before I listened to the same sequence of lectures. Spiro's exceptionally legible and profuse note-taking bore so many exact phrases just as they appeared in my own material, and the structure of the lectures followed so closely what my own evidence supplied, that I feel confirmed in my initial conviction that this was a series of talks that Hartz delivered, virtually unchanged, for a quarter of a century.

Professor Sanford A. Lakoff of the Department of Political Science at the University of California, San Diego, also a former student of Hartz, read the final version of the manuscript and make numerous telling improvements. I also owe a special thank you to Irving Louis Horowitz. His faith in my undertaking this task of scholarly reconstruction has helped keep me convinced of the merits of the proposal, and he has made useful suggestions that have improved the final result.

In understanding the background to *The Necessity of Choice:*

Nineteenth-Century Political Thought it is essential to keep in mind that Hartz originally worked out these thoughts in the years immediately following the conclusion of World War II. He was dealing with Western political thinking still under the shadow of the successful completion of the war against European dictators like Hitler and Mussolini. That military triumph had been preceded, however, by two decades in which democratic systems seemed to have developed unexpected difficulties in coping with various stresses and strains of twentieth-century political life. Even though earlier liberal theorists would have been surprised at the fragility of modern democratic regimes, at the same time Hartz was living in a period when Josef Stalin's power in the Soviet Union and Eastern Europe was reaching unrivalled proportions. If from our point of view Hartz sometimes seems awfully tough on Karl Marx, despite Hartz's own conceptual indebtedness to him, it is well to remember what were then thought of as the dangers of totalitarianism.

In trying to rebuild the context in which Hartz first developed his political theories, I feel it is important to note that he had never felt drawn to Marxism in the way, for example, that either Daniel J. Boorstin or the eminent literary critic F. O. Matthiessen, among many others, had. Hartz was, to be sure, broadly influenced by Marx, and often saw ideas as the expression of class conflicts; but he notably insisted on the ethical objective of the autonomy of intellectual life, and the necessity of individual choice as an essential ingredient of liberty. At his graduation from Harvard College Hartz had been awarded a travelling fellowship, which because of the start of World War II he could not take in Europe. Instead he went to Latin America, and I recall him telling me how he had once known someone then in Mexico who was passionately devoted to Leon Trotsky's *History of the Russian Revolution.* Hartz said he asked to borrow the book, but his request was granted on a condition: that it be returned after a single night. Hartz never forgot the religious significance that that text had for its owner.

At the time an American liberal had every reason to be immensely proud of the successes of Franklin D. Roosevelt's New Deal. Hartz had just lived through one of the most glorious periods in the history of American liberalism, characterized by intelligence being mobilized by those in power for the sake of social rearrangements. His first book, *Economic Policy and Democratic Thought: Pennsylvania, 1776–1860*, was an implicit confirmation of the New Deal belief that laissez-faire practices in early America were a myth.[27] Other typical features of the New Deal outlook can be found in *The Necessity of Choice*. A certain instrumentalism shows up; Hartz is apt, perhaps under the influence of Thorstein Veblen and his idealization of the model of engineers, to romanticize the way values can be successfully carried out in action. Hartz seems to share an attitude that sometimes borders on naive problem-solving, but the ideas he talks about were more apt to appear like weapons in social action then than they do now. It is the metaphors in Hartz's language that I am drawing attention to, in order to help keep readers reasonably sympathetic to the lines of thought that will be developing in this book.

Hartz had an extraordinary skill in dramatizing conflicts in modern political theory. Although I myself had occasion as a student to listen to brilliant lectures by famous teachers in the field, like Sir Isaiah Berlin and others as well, Hartz's presentations as a lecturer still stand out in my mind for his ability to weave a powerful consecutive flow of a structured argument. On individual thinkers he could perhaps be unfair, and careful observers of the history of political ideas will find faults with some separate parts of what Hartz was trying to establish. Were he alive today, doubtless he would have revised many of his individual points in the light of modern scholarship. Despite flaws in his argument which today's experts will be able to find, Hartz was all along basically using history for the sake of eliciting answers to some theoretical queries in connection with the nature of a free society; and these fundamental issues remain with us today. He did have an exceptional overall vision of the period, and it is to the success of his sweep in working that out that I would like to call attention.

Hartz has been known mostly as the author of *The Liberal Tradition in America*. "Rich in learning and powerfully argued, Hartz's book captured the imagination of a generation of students of American culture."[28] Over the past thirty-five years a secondary literature about Hartz's work, not all of it entirely favorable, has developed.[29] In others writing about Hartz, some attention has been paid to the comparative historical perspective that he brought to his study of American political thought. Yet almost no care has been given to Hartz as an interpreter of European political thought, or how it might bear on his understanding of America.

In fact Hartz only came to his study of American thought from a broad interest in the nature of liberal society in general. Many of the names that crop up briefly in *The Liberal Tradition in America* get more extended treatment in *The Necessity of Choice*. Hartz approached "the concept of a liberal society,"[30] which appears at the outset of *The Liberal Tradition in America,* only after having been steeped for years in the entire history of Western political philosophy.

Hartz's fundamental ethical commitments remained those of a troubled liberal. In the immediate post-World War II years he felt embattled against all theories of historical inevitability, and he sought to work out an approach to liberty in society which could be defined in terms of what he called "meaningful choice." Yet he refused to work only in the realm of philosophic abstractions, but sought to ground all his arguments in individual theories as they had been historically advanced.

At the height of the Vietnam war he testified on the nature of revolution before the Senate Foreign Relations Committee, and then expressed a position on the distinction between facts and values that is pertinent to the argument of *The Necessity of Choice:*

> What I am saying is that the value of liberty seems to be to me a value to be generally applied. When liberty does not exist in a society even though the history of that society has been different from the history of any we may be familiar with, I say that that society is open to criticism because liberty is not present in it. On the other hand, and here we come down to what seems to be the root of the matter, what we have to do is to disentangle our faith in the norm of freedom from the peculiar historical experience in which it has been cast in the United States. We have to be able to distinguish the universality of an ethic from the peculiar framework in which we have received it. Once we do this, then we are embarked on a perfectly realistic path. We have a value, we have a norm by which we can evaluate social

situations, even foreign social situations. We are not morally adrift. We have not surrendered to the idea that anything is as good as anything else and any culture is as good as any other culture. We have not sunk to complete relativity. But at the same time we are not demanding of other cultures that they instantly become like ourselves. We are willing to realize that the norm of liberty can fulfill itself in many different ways. . . .[31]

Throughout the *Necessity of Choice* Hartz will be engaged in combatting a variety of deterministic viewpoints, each of which amounted to evasions of responsibility; he valued the essential ethical attractiveness of liberty yet appreciated the empirical validity of the challenges it faced. He continued to seek to retain a realm of moral autonomy. It is my hope that this book will communicate some of the excitement that came from an encounter with his powerful mind in action, and help ensure his stature within modern social thought.

Notes

1. Louis Hartz, *The Liberal Tradition in America: An Interpretation of American Political Thought Since the Revolution* (N.Y., Harcourt Brace & Co., 1955).
2. Cf. Hartz's testimony before Senator Fulbright's committee during the Vietnam war. U.S. Congress. Senate. Committee on Foreign Relations. *Hearings: The Nature of Revolution.* 90th Congress, 2nd session (Feb. 26, 1968), 109–52. I am indebted to N. Gordon Levin for bringing this presentation by Hartz to my attention.
3. David Riesman, with Nathan Glazer and Reuel Denney, *The Lonely Crowd* (New Haven, Yale Univ. Press, 1950).
4. David Riesman, *Individualism Reconsidered and Other Essays* (Glencoe, Il., The Free Press, 1954).
5. Lionel Trilling, *The Liberal Imagination: Essays on Literature and Society* (N.Y., Viking Press, 1950).
6. Hartz, *Liberal Tradition in America,* 6.
7. Ibid., 9.
8. Ibid., 10.
9. Ibid., 12.
10. Ibid., 14.
11. Adrienne Koch and William Peden, eds., *The Life and Selected Writings of Thomas Jefferson* (N.Y., The Modern Library, 1944), 322.
12. Hartz, *Liberal Tradition in America,* 20.
13. Louis Hartz, "The Rise of the Democratic Idea," in *Paths of American Thought,* ed. Arthur M. Schlesinger, Jr. and Morton

White (Boston, Houghton Mifflin, 1963), 37–51; and Louis Hartz, "Comment," *Comparative Studies in Society and History* 5, no. 3 (April 1963), 279–84.

14. George Fitzhugh, *Cannibals All! or Slaves Without Masters,* ed. C. Vann Woodward (Cambridge, Harvard Univ. Press, 1960), ix.
15. Hartz, *Liberal Tradition in America,* 192.
16. Ibid., 156–57, 176.
17. Richard Hofstadter, *The Progressive Historians: Turner, Beard, and Parrington* (N.Y., Knopf, 1968), 448.
18. John Higham, "The Cult of the 'American Consensus': Homogenizing Our History," *Commentary,* 28 (Feb. 1959), 95–96.
19. Daniel J. Boorstin, "Review of Hartz's *The Liberal Tradition in America,*" *Commentary,* 20, no. 1 (July 1955), 99–100.
20. Marvin Meyers, "Louis Hartz, *The Liberal Tradition in America:* An Appraisal," *Comparative Studies in Society and History,* 5, no. 3 (April 1963), 264.
21. Louis Hartz, "Democracy: Image and Reality," in *Democracy in the Mid-Twentieth Century* (St. Louis, Mo., Washington Univ. Press, 1960), 13–29; also in *Democracy Today: Problems and Perspectives,* ed. William N. Chambers and Robert H. Salisbury (N.Y., Collier Books, 1963), 25–44.
22. Louis Hartz, *The Founding of New Societies: Studies in the History of the U.S., Latin America, South Africa, Canada & Australia* (N.Y., Harcourt Brace & World, 1964).
23. Cf. Gad Horowitz, "Conservatism, Liberalism, and Socialism in Canada: An Interpretation," *Canadian Journal of Economics and Political Science,* 32 (1966), 143–71; H. D. Forbes, "Hartz-Horowitz at Twenty: Nationalism, Toryism & Socialism in Canada and the U.S.," *Canadian Journal of Political Science,* 20 (1987), 287–315; James Holt, "Louis Hartz's Fragment Thesis," *New Zealand Journal of History,* 7, no. 1 (April 1973), 3–11; and Luca Meldolesi, "America, America: note su Hirschman, Hartz & Braudel," *Inchiesta* (Luglio–Settembre 1985), 1–15.
24. Louis Hartz, *A Synthesis of World History* (Zurich, Humanity, 1984). Cf. Patrick Riley, "Louis Hartz: The Final Years, The Unknown Work," *Political Theory,* 16, no. 3 (August 1988), 377–99.
25. John Patrick Diggins, *The Lost Soul of American Politics: Virtue, Self-Interest, and the Foundations of Liberalism* (N.Y., Basic Books, 1984). See also John Patrick Diggins, "Knowledge and Sorrow: Louis Hartz's Quarrel with American History," *Political Theory,* 16, no. 3 (August 1988), 355–76.
26. David Margolick, "Obituary of Louis Hartz," *New York Times,* 24 Jan. 1986. See also Samuel H. Beer, "Louis Hartz: In Memoriam," *PS,* Summer 1986, 735–37.
27. Louis Hartz, *Economic Policy and Democratic Thought: Pennsylvania, 1776–1860* (Cambridge, Harvard Univ. Press, 1948).

28. Daniel Walker Howe, "European Sources of Political Ideas in Jeffersonian America," in *The Promise of American History: Progress and Prospects,* ed. Stanley I. Kutler and Stanley N. Katz (Baltimore, Johns Hopkins University Press, 1982), 28.

29. See, for example, Marian J. Morton, *The Terrors of Ideological Politics: Liberal Historians in a Conservative Mood* (Cleveland, Case Western Reserve Press, 1972); Bernard Sternsher, *Consensus, Conflict, and American Historians* (Bloomington, Indiana Univ. Press, 1975); Richard H. Pells, *The Liberal Mind in a Conservative Age: American Intellectuals in the 1940s and 1950s* (N.Y., Harper & Row, 1985); J. G. A. Pocock, *The Machiavellian Moment: Florentine Political Thought and the Atlantic Republican Tradition* (Princeton, Princeton Univ. Press, 1975); Thomas L. Pangle, *The Spirit of Modern Republicanism: The Moral Vision of the American Founders and the Philosophy of Locke* (Chicago, Univ. of Chicago Press, 1988); and Robert A. Packenham, *Liberal America and the Third World* (Princeton, Princeton Univ. Press, 1973).

30. Hartz, *Liberal Tradition in America,* 3.

31. *Hearings: The Nature of Revolution,* 133.

Part I

THE REVOLUTIONARY BACKGROUND

1

Origins

The origins of the French Revolution is the essential place to begin to understand ninteenth-century political theory, for the great revolution itself became the main issue during at least the first half of the century. Throughout almost all European countries two institutional systems had been competing against each other: in France before 1789 royal absolutism, after an ancient struggle, coexisted with the surviving remnants of feudalism. The monarchy, while still seeking to extend itself, had been confronted by the persistence of a quasi-feudal structure. The social dualism consisted of aspiring monarchs locked in an unresolved conflict with this traditionalist regime. Although French society was deeply divided, such institutional tension was historically not an abnormal situation, and the country was not inevitably bound to collapse in an upheaval. Any isolating of powerful social divisions should merely become the starting point of sound political analysis.

Certain basic institutional assumptions, which also reflected contrasting ambitions, were implicit in the simultaneous existence of these two competing rival forces. The central image of authority was that of a great social chain in which power resided in many places. The monarchy was at the apex of a system of distributed power. Yet the king who presided did not create such multiplicity nor could he subordinate it; he was incapable of being commanding enough to control the ancien régime. The monarchy derived its authority, like the Church and the communes too, from a thoroughly decentralized system.

A fundamental difference persisted over the proper locus of power in society. Class formed one center, each one with separate claims of its own. The nobility and monarchy generally shared power, without there yet being a distinction between public and private realms; a fusion of private patrimony and public authority had been characteristic of feudalism. And from the territorial angle, decentralized foci of power were authoritative: cities, for example, had their own traditions and peculiarities, with claims to ancient liberties; provincial as well as municipal independence meant that the French monarchy had to continue to struggle against such communal power. Finally, corporate entities, such as the Church, guilds, and universities, functioned in their own right, independently of any central authority, in furthering the complex decentralization of the old feudal system. Whole series of corporations claimed the authority of self-government, with their own taxes to levy and even separate courts. In all the Catholic countries the Church had a tremendous power base, especially in Spain with its separate ecclesiastical jurisdiction that was more important than the civil authority.

The ancien régime's philosophical outlook rejected above all the proposition of sovereignty. Instead of legitimacy being derived from the state, power was viewed as inherently diffuse, held by different elements of the system separately. The monarch was the presiding officer of a structure it could not dominate.

The twentieth-century guild socialists in England (such as Harold Laski, G. D. H. Cole, and J. N. Figgis in the 1920s) would glorify the decentralized system in pre-Revolutionary Europe, for it would seem glamorous as a corporate society which did not value rampant individualism. According to the prevailing social myth, each person then viewed himself in terms of a larger whole—a class, a corporation, or a province. Everyone was indissolubly associated with a corporate, local, or class grouping; these social institutions defined one's place and provided support, assuming responsibility for the individual. Each person was not lonely but rooted in a context providing security and purpose.

At the same time the pre-Revolutionary era was not a tyrannical situation. Power was so pluralized that the entire weight of social authority could never be mustered against an individual. The pluralistic system was so diverse and multiple that Karl Marx would later romanticize in his *Communist Manifesto* about the "numberless chartered freedoms" in that early time. The individual retained the capacity to move between types of power centers. In the twentieth century it is now possible to mobilize society in a totalitarian fashion; but that earlier period still had a decentralization and looseness about its social joints. "Liberty is ancient," Madame de Stael would declare after the French Revolution, "despotism is modern."

The ancien régime never fulfilled the ideal image associated with its myth. By the eighteenth century the system had seriously deteriorated in terms of its moral purposes. Each instrument of the feudal power structure had become tightly oligarchical; the Church and the guilds, for instance, had turned into vehicles of vested interests. As such rigidities were imposed on individuals, the social response was revolution.

The corporate feudal system remained in conflict with monarchical power, which ever since the sixteenth century had been aiming at unified authority in the hands of the state. The instinctive drift of monarchical activity had been the consolidation and centralization of power. The monarchy implicitly sought to shatter the corporatist outlook on life and to drain its power. In the contest between unity and plurality, monarchs sought the individualizing and equalizing of people.

The novel proposition that individuals are genuinely autonomous, and equal within the state, meant that human beings could successfully become unraveled from the meaning of their prior associations. Formerly corporate attachments had defined personality; in the breakdown of the old order individuals would be redefined. Each person began to exist not because of class or territory, but as an individual in the state, whether it be France or Prussia.

In France, the royal *intendants,* for example, began to decide disputes between the nobles and peasants. Being an aristocrat or a peasant was in itself ceasing to be meaningful, as they both stood together before a central authority. Class distinctions remained as ever, yet on one level of existence the two litigants were now both just legal contestants. The royal bureaucracy began successfully to invade the old chaotic, decentralized regime, undermining the ties of status, locality, and class. Individuals ceased to be members of local corporations, they were disengaged from old structures, and they became citizens of the state. The centralization of power became, therefore, linked with new forms of individualism.

Americans, however, basically think that unified authority must be a threat to the individual. Yet historically monarchical despotism was the agent for liberating people and making them equal in the face of common state power; the centralization of power was the instrument for the creation of individualism— indeed individuality. Nowadays we live in a time when the monarchical impulse has been in great degree victorious. The idea of state sovereignty and equal citizenship is part of our post-Revolutionary mythology. We do not easily remember that the state, as it destroyed corporate society, was once the ally of the individual. By the time the state exists alongside equal individuals, detached from their corporate allegiances, it then becomes a threat to the individual; the state, in liberating people from the Church, for example, can itself come to be a danger.

In the United States we never confronted the same task as in Europe, since the old corporate order had never been transported across the Atlantic. The state from the outset in America was defined as potentially threatening to individualism. America was created in terms of categories of political thought when the danger of the state alone existed, and we have therefore never been able to conceive of the liberating qualities of the state. Flight from Europe obliterated the many built-in social antagonisms to the state. Here the state arose easily, without the need to triumph over a corporate order, and consequently from the outset was viewed as an enemy to freedom. European experience indicates how the state need not only be a coercive threat, but can also be a friend. Traditional attitudes to the police in Britain, for example, reflect a basically different orientation toward the politics of the state than in America.

All over Western Europe the tension between the two systems, monarchical and the quasi-feudal order, persisted. The success of either side varied, from country to country and within countries. The conflict was never resolved, neither system really won, and a stalemate was reached. In France the monarchy scored an apparent success. It drastically challenged the old chaotic system; yet beyond a certain point the monarchy seemed hamstrung in its attempt to conquer the wilderness of corporate decentralized society. Notably, Anne-Robert-Jacques Turgot failed in his program of radical reform, as he was blocked by corporate society. The monarchy appeared to lose its will to master this scheme, and solve its problem. The reason for this failure was partly due to the resistance of the system; but in addition the monarchy had a special defect of its own. It lost its self-confidence because it was a part of the system under attack; hereditary rule was too similar to the ultimate rationale for the traditionalistic order itself. After invading the customary ethos of the corporate order, it found that it was damaging the roots of its own legitimacy. The men who ultimately succeeded in liquidating the corporate system were to be those not wedded to the philosophy of the ancien régime: the French revolutionaries and Napoleon.

In the clash of forces between two apparently different outlooks a single primary moral premise bound them together, and therefore neither could be entirely victorious. Is a deeply divided society necessarily ready for revolt? It would be highly superficial to assume that because a battle is unresolved there is a danger of revolution. The coexistence of old and new systems is always socially present, as illustrated, for example, in Leon Trotsky's Law of Combined Development. It is not the overlapping of regimes by itself that is potentially dangerous.

In France the role of the middle class became critical for the revolution. The dualism, the unconsummated conflict, was made a threat to the social system by virtue of its association with other things happening. As Niccolo Machiavelli taught, it is fine to go all the way, but if you move only halfway it is often better not to have proceeded at all. This principle is applicable to certain activities of the French monarchy. In its efforts to undermine the aristocracy, the monarchy also eliminated much of its own political and juridical power locally. Meanwhile the privileges of the nobility remained and even increased. The monarchy made the corporate structure more intolerable as a consequence of undermining its power but leaving its privileges intact.

As Alexis de Tocqueville knew, the tendency to divorce power from privilege was critical in France, and led to an explosive situation. The impulse of the monarchy was to create parasitism, always a dangerous political phenomenon. Privilege, without the responsibilities and authority of office, makes for revolutionary possibilities. Resentment is not a universal capacity; people have to be capable of it. Revolution will not occur when the public is so downtrodden that it cannot articulate grievances; revolution requires self-confidence and security. In France plenty of such self-assurance existed. It was the most prosperous country in Europe, as both its peasants and middle class were thriving. These self-confident social forces, observing the resolution of the dualistic conflict in the creation of parasitism, expressed a sense of outrage and righteous indignation.

For example, the peasant confronted the royal bureaucrat as the determinant of his fate. The peasant was comparatively well-off, and had been acquiring land for over a generation. But he had to continue to pay dues to his noble, and under the new conditions such payment was felt as worse than before. The peasant saw the monarchy as deciding what was happening to him, yet continued to make financial contributions to a nonfunctioning, now powerless aristocrat. To the extent that the peasant had optimism and hope, based on owning some land, he became the more dangerous.

But the middle class proved decisive, and provides the clue to the course of the nineteenth century. It was made up of an assortment of elements in society that had been thrown up to new power and self-confidence. The middle class had been left out of the central contest and was not included in the classical categories. It had no institutionalized forms of expression. Because of its noninclusion in the social struggle, the middle class studied the whole foundations of the situation. Sociologically it was amorphous and heterogeneous. At its core were merchants and financiers who had begun to develop tremendous authority and power, but it also contained a motley group of professional men, members of the royal bureaucracy, and rich master craftsmen.

This middle class generated its own pressure against the ancien régime. The bureaucrats were biased against the corporate scheme anyway. The monarchs, too, disliked the territorial tolls, and wanted a unified national trading area. From a commercial point of view provincialism hampered trade. The Church seemed to be extracting unnecessary money, and its land-ownership withdrew large areas from the possibility of capitalist enterprise. The guilds also seemed to control too much of the labor power. The middle class disliked the fusion of privilege and lack of power, and wanted the nobility closed down because of its esprit de corps.

The middle class was wondering about the social drama as a whole; witnessing the struggle it chose one side, and subsequently the middle class did not give up its faith in the monarchy easily. Very patiently it hoped that royal absolutism would succeed in liberating it from the frustrations of the old system. But the middle class failed to realize the inherent limitations of the monarchy and the degree to which it was intertwined with the system it was fighting. The middle class endured the failures of Turgot and the monarchy; well after 1789 it still stuck by the monarchy. Royal absolutism remained the ideal. Although Jean-Jacques Rousseau gave up faith in the monarchy, that decision would come late for the middle class.

The main body of the philosophes throughout the mid-eighteenth century adhered to a common core of ideas; the Enlightenment flourished thanks to the intellectual spearheading from the French middle class. Antoine-Nicholas de Condorcet and Paul Henri Holbach did come from the nobility, but the largest percentage of the other writers (such as Francois Marie Voltaire, Rousseau, and Denis Diderot) came from the middle class. There was no problem converting them to middle class ideas, since they themselves instinctively expressed them with the supreme self-confidence of a group which has made its own way.

They all shared an immense curiosity about their environment. As enemies of their society they had a problem of survival, and were forced to manipulate their world by means of exploiting the tensions within the system. They were opponents of the Church, and made use of the king's own aversion to it, especially under Madame Pompadour; so they attacked the Church in aid of the monarchy. The censorship against them was loose and as David Hume pointed out, weak censorship whets the appetite and provides a special quality of excitement. Certain sections of nobility supported the philosophes, and these enemies of their society were able to thrive. No real opposition existed within the system, and therefore the philosophes emerged as the central critics. They maneuvered within the interstices of their society. They were opposed to the status quo yet had no practical experience, and were devoid of the responsibilities of governing. The situation would differ radically in the American Revolution; Rousseau can be contrasted with John Adams, who wrote the iconoclastic literature of one who has held power.

The middle class had chosen to give its loyalties to the monarchy; and from its initial stages of the French Enlightenment absolutism was linked to liberty. The monarchy was accepted as the potential liberator of the middle class from the oppressions of the corporate order, in behalf of individualizing and equalizing people as citizens. Until the middle class lost faith in the monarchy, the philosophes (except for Diderot, Rousseau, and Condorcet) would articulate the basic impulses of royal aims.

In the struggle of royal absolutism against the corporate society of the eighteenth century, the philosophes as spokesmen for the middle class relied on the monarchy to destroy the ancien régime. The essential fusion of absolutism and freedom can be found in the thought of the philosophes. The state was the weapon chosen to clear away the old society, to free it from the burden of the corporate structure; and the goal for the use of the monarchy was the liberation of the individual. Unlimited power and freedom, then, became an instinctive pair of concepts in Enlightenment thinking, and this union of apparent opposites played its part in the historical beginnings of modern liberal thought.

2

The Religious Problem

The Enlightenment alliance between absolutism and the friends of liberty can be illustrated by Voltaire's treatise on tolerance. He had a passion for toleration and yet he did not really develop a philosophy of it. Voltaire's position was polemical and limited in its implications, a response to a specific situation. Two aspects of the British tradition of thought on the same subject were lacking. First, no psychological or epistemological basis for toleration, as in John Locke, was spelled out. Toleration was not defended in relativistic terms, that is, the view that since individual experience is different, a variety of religious beliefs becomes necessary, and therefore toleration is desirable. Second, both John Milton's *Areopagitica* and John Stuart Mill's *On Liberty* share a version of the marketplace of ideas concept of truth: the reasoning that since each individual contributes to a larger truth, everyone should be treated as if what they express contains a grain of merit.

Voltaire was not concerned with this British line of thought, and instead developed the concept of natural right negatively. It was not due to confusion on his part, but rather to the limited degree to which he was philosophically concerned with the problem. He is even vague on toleration as a natural right; instead he declared that "one does not have a natural right to be intolerant." His argument is an example of the lack of philosophic depth in the philosophes. Although the energy behind their formulations was undeniable, in the realm of deep explorations these men failed. Their talents were journalistic, and they succeeded as brilliant expositors of their beliefs.

Voltaire believed that diversity of opinion will not undermine society, but give the state more stability. Liberty of thought was held by him to be useful. He proposed to shatter any universal convictions, since the religious coercions of the day rested on the unity of beliefs. Voltaire thought that the liberty of expression that he advocated would not weaken society, and that a multiplicity of sects, with the free play of conviction, would in the end produce stability.

While Voltaire was arguing this way in the religious sphere, Montesquieu was also impressed with English liberty politically. His insight in the political field was similar to Voltaire's views on religion. Montesquieu thought that the balance and diversity of the English constitution contained checks on despotism, restraints on the fanaticism of any single branch of government. While Voltaire was advocating variety in religious convictions, Montesquieu argued in behalf of multiplicity in political institutions. Montesquieu thus wrote in favor of the separation of powers and political plurality. Voltaire might seem to have agreed, since his arguments for diversity in the religious sphere were similar.

The philosophes, however, did not approve of Montesquieu. In some sense he had carried forward Voltaire's pluralistic ideas. Yet the enthusiasm of Voltaire for religious diversity did not carry over into his views on political life. The philosophes did not agree that liberty was ensured by institutional multiplicity.

Voltaire assailed the idea of checks and balances. Montesquieu's *The Spirit of the Laws* was not congenial to Helvetius or Turgot either. They attacked him because his scheme lacked unity of power; it was a period of extreme theories of sovereignty. The Enlightenment passion for toleration was associated with absolutism; the monarchy was the weapon chosen to dissolve religious coercions and to liberate the individual. Political unity was needed to weaken the Church and to limit clerical authority in order to establish religious liberty. Therefore theories of absolute sovereignty were worked out; singular power was linked to social freedom. The dissolution of corporate society could only be accomplished by political absolutism.

Montesquieu's reasoning reminded them of the old corporate society. They had had enough of pluralized power, which sounded reactionary. It was in fact a sound instinct on the part of the philosophes, since Montesquieu had a love of French history and tradition that they lacked.

The argument in behalf of religious toleration was tied to the need for political unity. Eighteenth-century France bore resemblances to the sixteenth century, in that liberty was associated with absolutism. The doctrine of sovereignty (first proposed by Jean Bodin and the *politiques*) originally developed in France as an ally of liberty. The initial defense of the state forms part of the history of liberalism. Until only recently the state, the substitute for the old feudal order, was viewed as an ally of freedom. Bodin's own theory leads directly to the work of the philosophes. The image underlying their reasoning can also be found in Thomas Hobbes, who contrasted sovereign power and the isolated individual; Locke too related the equality and freedom of the individual with the state. Any pluralized situation seemed opposed to the growth of individual liberty.

Montesquieu perceived the tragedy of the situation; for he saw that despotism promotes both monotony and individuality. While Montesquieu denounced the individualizing and egalitarian aspects of absolutism, Voltaire applauded it. Montesquieu objected to despotism because all individuals are the same in relation to the sovereign, but that is what Voltaire and his allies wanted. John Stuart Mill also later complained about the lack of individualism in democracy. But why should anyone have worried about this in the eighteenth century? Yet what these thinkers failed to consider by virtue of the intensity with which they approached the problem of the dissolution of the old society, other ages had to deal with. For when the state becomes the recipient of all this authority, there can be no assurance that it will not become tyrannical and as intolerant as the Church. The philosophes were so engaged with fighting the Church, for example, that their preoccupation obscured the potential dangers of a liberated state. Implicit was the notion that the state would leave things alone. The ideal of toleration could only be sustained with the help of the optimistic hope that the despot will always be enlightened. The state was emerging as the receptacle of all power in the alliance between absolutism and liberty.

Voltaire's demand for toleration was part of the vast undermining of Catholic theology. The concepts of reason and nature, most characteristic of eighteenth-century thought, were the tools for weakening the hold of Catholicism. From the perspective of the Church, notions of rationalism and natural law were not created by people like Voltaire, Turgot, and Helvetius. The concepts of reason and nature go back to ancient stoicism and Roman Law. These ideas also came out of an old tradition in Catholic theology itself; ever since St. Thomas Aquinas they were central to Catholic thinking. Eighteenth-century thought was an aspect of a long-term secularizing drive, and the Church had the problem of adjusting itself to the rationalism of the era.

In Aquinas's system natural law was subordinate to divine law. By the eighteenth-century natural law was made an independent source of ethical obligation to provide a guide for the conduct and morality of individual men. Theologians within the Church wanted to adapt to their own time. Natural law can be held to be an independent source of morality, yet for theologians this is easier said than done. For if reason and nature become separate origins of obligation, then what becomes of the special role of revelation or even the Church itself?

Puritanical elements within the Church, Jansenism, arose against the liberalized tendency in the Church, and resisted the new rationalism. The Jansenists reverted to a pre-Thomistic, Augustinian line of thought, as they battled within the Church against the new extreme of rationalism and humanism. In a polarized theological situation the Jansenists adhered to a new extremism, the fanaticism of living by a reliance on revelation. Without divine law there can be no revelation, but otherwise, they reasoned, there would be no Church. Within Voltaire's own attack on intolerance there had been a response to both wings of Catholicism. The Church and the philosophes were together in the grip of a new rationalizing drive. The fresh categories of the struggle presented the Church with an insoluble dilemma; if it failed to accommodate itself the Church set itself athwart the spirit of the age. Strategically the Church was right to adjust to the new climate of opinion.

The philosophes had the choice between looking at natural law empirically, as a Newtonian-like phenomenon, or normatively, in line with Aquinas's approach. The philosophes opted to be the crudest sorts of empiricists in their use of nature; under the influence of Newtonian science they were concerned with the discovery of uniformities in empirical nature. To answer the question whether miracles exist, they demanded that people examine the available evidence. Yet their insistence on such verification had some curious implications. For if the concept of a miracle was blasted by the empirical facts of the matter, it was at the same time true that people had in fact long believed in miracles: France was a Catholic country with a feudal past.

Given their own commitment to empiricism the philosophes were half-hearted in the solution to their problem. If one accepts experience, and the significance of empirical reality, then the power of the Church and the belief in both revelation and miracles becomes a part of natural law. The philosophes were at heart frightened at remaining thorough-going empiricists; they would have discovered the uniformity of Catholicism in French experience. Gottfried Leibniz's doctrine maintained that this is a good world because natural law manifests itself in historical development; he was notably assailed by Voltaire in *Candide*. And Sir William Blackstone too complacently held to a best-of-all-possible-worlds line of thought. Conservatives thought that natural law unfolded itself in empirical experience. Montesquieu had adopted a version of Blackstone's position in maintaining that the meaning of nature could be found in the flow of French history.

The philosophes started out, then, as insistent empiricists when dealing with the issue of existence of miracles; but they were frightened by the implications of any actual beliefs in miracles, and therefore shifted to using natural law in a normative sense. The concept of nature became an ethical standard by which empirical institutions were to be judged. Nature was taken from earth and placed in heaven to evaluate experience. Natural law became an ethical standard by which institutions were to be assessed, thanks to the defect of nerve of the philosophes in their use of nature as an empirical concept.

Why were the philosophes so frightened by the prospect of the implications of uncompromising empiricism? Blackstone and Montesquieu had been empiricists but also conservatives; their defense of the status quo came from an inversion of the same fallacy of the philosophes. Blackstone thought that because historical facts existed they were necessarily good; he confused a fact with a norm. After all, the existence of something need not justify it. The philosophes assumed that natural law was normative out of the fear of a hidden justification in the empirical past.

There is a crucial difference between a fact and a judgment on it, which neither the philosophes nor these conservatives appreciated. The philosophes had only to affirm that no fact will logically entail any norm, and thereby they could afford to look all facts in the face. But they were troubled by the underlying conviction that they would have to accept conservative conclusions to empiricism. They were taken in by their fears of historicism. David Hume had earlier dissolved naive natural law reasoning; any systematic approach to theology need not necessitate acceptance. But Hume's argument was ignored in eighteenth-century France; even had they read Hume, they would not have accepted his insight because of their strategic social purposes.

If the philosophes had been consistent empiricists, they would have discovered both that miracles do not happen and that France was traditionally a Catholic country. A broader truth was that every society has some myth, or system of symbols, which binds it powerfully together. Voltaire talks as if religion only started with Christianity, and the ancient Greeks and the Indians never existed. But the mere presence of Catholicism in France need not have prevented the philosophes from anything—even being atheists. Religion should have been seen as a part of the inevitable symbolic system that helps hold a society together, a kind of Platonic myth. Yet they need not have accepted this particular function of religion.

Because objects fall at a certain rate we do not have to submit to anything. Similarly, the discovery of social uniformity does not prevent a high degree of radicalism. The philosophes could have substituted a new myth, a new religion; they could have confronted the problem of how to construct a new set of symbols to destroy the old. But they thought they had to yield to what they had discovered. They might even have devised a system in which no myth at all existed, although this would have been hard. In such a new rationalistic worldview symbolism would have been unnecessary.

But they embarked on neither of these approaches. Since the facts frightened them they evolved deism; they proposed a cold rationalistic philosophy rather than a substitute theology. A doctrine of a prime mover was not possible for the masses. They could have tried making a myth out of the state, as in ancient Greece or China; they could have channeled authority from the Church to the state, around which a new myth would center. But they did not opt for this alternative either. The monarchy in their system was as cold, impersonal, and rational as the prime mover; it seemed no more humanly warm than the first cause of deism, and they did not dramatize the king. They really robbed the monarch of the mythical qualities he had in the seventeenth century. Carl Becker once argued that they denatured God and deified nature; there is some truth in the idea that nature became God for the philosophes. But it was not accurate in terms of political theory, since nature was not conceived symbolically as a myth.

The philosophes failed to confront the real problem of the meaning of religious experience in society. They took flight to a normative use of nature when sociological facts were encountered. Reform objectives could have been met, but this did not happen. There was no logical necessity to their limit on empirical observation; the desire for reform can be accompanied by realism. (One need only to think of the modern Brandeis brief.) They were frightened of the concept of nature and made a strategic mistake. It was not just a philosophical confusion on their part; it would be a big error to think them too unenlightened.

Their basic problem was historical. Had they gone into a sociology of religion, they would have had to recognize the necessity of dealing with the empirical existence of the Church.

They did not see things in this light because of a desire to avoid the issue. They had the task of thinking through the implications of intellectual freedom, but that meant a constructive problem of examining the idea of liberty in a social context.

As revolutionaries they were interested in destruction. It takes a constructive passion to create a new Church or to propose no Church, and that would be asking too much of them. It is impossible to expect a radical also to be a bureaucrat and a constructive thinker as well. The philosophes were using empiricism to undermine the old order at the same time that they evaded the issue of sociology. When it came to building a new society they flew to the sky. The concept of nature was a handy device for accomplishing their aim. They reasoned myth out of existence in the course of logically assailing the Church. They were thereby enabled to entertain the idea of intellectual freedom apart from sociological facts. For Voltaire liberty was a disembodied norm. He had no realism as to how to implement freedom in society, or any understanding of the social meaning of religion.

The philosophes did have general alternatives open to them. They could have accepted the corporate society, just asking for more power for the middle class within the preexisting framework. Like New Dealers they might have offered to work within the system. Instead they made a frontal attack on the Church in behalf of atheism and deism. They could also have opposed the old corporate society, and tried to create a new social system. But they did not want to confront the problem of developing a new myth or religion. So in the end what they did was reason the problem of society out of existence entirely; this was the course they pursued, which left a vacuum which would later be filled by the French revolutionaries. The philosophes proposed, in affirming their norms, to use natural law to smash society; but they would not investigate the implementing of their values in a real social context. Society was implicitly reasoned down the drain, since it was ignored and dissolved by the flight to an abstract norm. The natural law concept became the banner by which the old society was assailed and a new order prevented from arising.

3

The Economic Question

Throughout the works of physiocratic thinkers, such as François Quesnay, Du Pont de Nemours, and Turgot, there is no immediate sense of polemics. Voltaire's literary violence strikingly contrasts with the placidity of Quesnay. This school of thought was a sober attempt at economic science; it represents the genesis of modern economics. The basic query of the physiocrats concerning the economic world was, what is the source of economic productivity? That they asked this question is the clue to the assumptions of their theory, for it was an implicit challenge to the noneconomic premises underlying corporate society with its nonacquisitive values. The ancien régime's theology was otherworldly, concerned with salvation; feudalism enshrined the significance of status, norms of honor and military prowess; nobility was identified, as Thorstein Veblen pointed out, with conspicuous waste. Therefore the consequences of the physiocratic query were explosive. To ask quite soberly what is the source of economic productivity was to launch a profound attack, a utilitarian blast, for the physiocrats were taking for granted the dissolution of old values. To assume the irrelevance of outmoded standards was bound to be infuriating.

The answer of the physiocrats was that land is the only source of productivity, and that agricultural effort is the only productive labor. All other nonagricultural forms of work were deemed sterile; the implication was that whole classes could be parasitic. The measure of productivity was not the creation of anything, but the achievement of a surplus; craftsmen used up all they created. Land alone, the physiocrats held, had the capacity to create a surplus.

According to physiocratic thinking, craftsmen and merchants are valuable and do necessary things; in physiocratic theory they produce that which is necessary for survival. Nonagricultural occupations had their functions; the physiocratic point was much like the later Marxian theory of the limited role of the machine, incapable of creating surplus either. To Marx, machinery deteriorates since it is supposedly a passive instrument. For the physiocrats surplus was defined as that which gets produced over and above what is consumed. And that was, they held, only possible by laboring on land. (Adam Smith in England would repudiate this idea.)

The nobility and the Church owned a great deal of land; they characteristically viewed it not in terms of economic exploitation but rather loosely as what could be gotten from it. Therefore vast tracts went to economic waste. This predominantly noneconomic orientation to the land contrasted with the physiocratic doctrine. The individual physiocrats came from the new group of landowners who were part of the middle class; large numbers of them were members of bureaucratic families in the royal service who used their funds for the purchase of land from old corporate proprietors and, unlike the nobility, they tried to work it capitalistically. This social situation was an inspiration for these theories about land.

The physiocratic obsession with land was also due to the overwhelmingly agricultural nature of France. Smith broadened productivity to other surplus activities, and included craftsmen and merchants. England was then a less agricultural society, and further ahead in the Industrial Revolution. But Smith retained the crucial physiocratic distinction between productivity and nonproductivity, which represented an attack on the old social system.

Physiocratic theory inaugurated a concept of searching for the economic parasite who does not produce but rather exploits the production of others. It subsequently runs through all modern thought, including that of David Ricardo. Here is the indirect origin of the Marxian doctrine of surplus value; the physiocratic concept of the exploitation of agricultural property by the rest of the economy is paralleled by the Marxian idea of the exploitation of the workers by owners. Starting with the physiocrats all men were looked on as economic personalities, not in terms of the old hierarchy of values. The distinction between an economically motivated personality and one who was not represented at the time a psychological revolution; it involved a vast departure from the old social order. To define personality in such a way took the individual out of the old corporate society and amounted to an ethical upheaval.

The tension between physiocratic theories and the old corporate order was not merely a matter of a clash in implicit values. For the physiocrats made a specific attack and demanded that concrete restrictions on economic activity be liquidated. This radical plea for economic liberty meant that trade restraint on freedom be dissolved. Turgot wrote in behalf of the liberty of workmen and against the guilds; others also attacked provincial tolls and demanded a national free trade area. The argument between the physiocrats and the social order of the eighteenth century was manifested in the issue of economic liberty. Physiocratic thinking was part of the attempt of liberals to unravel the individual from the restrictions of corporate society. The worker was to be defined in economic terms as an individual, a Frenchman who was no longer a member of a guild. The concept of an "apprentice shoemaker" was to be replaced by that of a Frenchman who might be making shoes.

This attack by the physiocrats was justified by natural law and natural rights, as was Voltaire's assault on religion. Each man had a natural right to economic freedom; as Locke theorized, liberty was justified in terms of anterior rights. Du Pont was unqualified in his assertion of this economic emancipation. But did the physiocratic position lead to notions of political freedom, a proposal for Lockian self-government through a fiduciary relationship between the people and the state? Montesquieu had proposed the separation of powers; but Voltaire and Helvetius, who defended absolutism, disagreed sharply with Montesquieu's idea of divided power. Du Pont in fact blasted the concept of checks and balances. The physiocratic demand for economic liberty followed the logic of associating the ideal of freedom with the defense of absolutism. The massive liberation of the individual by means of a despot was required by the need for the creation of a sharp instrument to dissolve the old order. Unified power was necessary to emancipate the individual.

As in discussing Voltaire, and the issue of what would happen to religious liberty after the Church was mastered, no assurance could exist that the liberating monarch would not be just as intolerant. Voltaire never confronted this matter in the course of defending the enlightened monarch. But the physiocrats could not avoid it entirely. For many specific economic restrictions came also from royal authority in its traditional form. The physiocrats assailed the corporations like the guilds and the Church, but were also opposed to mercantilism as a policy of the central government. The monarchy generated its own economic restrictions and therefore the problem of keeping it in bounds had to be faced. The physiocrats were preoccupied with how the monarch would behave, and therefore concerned with how to keep him confined once economic liberty was established. The problem of ensuring that a new sovereign will not become as tyrannical as ever once an old order is smashed is the dilemma of all revolutionaries, and revolutionary power becomes a threat once the previous regime is overcome. Although the physiocrats retained the dualism of absolutism and liberty, they had to probe the matter more deeply than Voltaire did.

They proposed to erect a body of magistrates, with the vague power of judicial review, to watch over the king and see that he behaved as a physiocratic monarch should. After having insisted on the unity of power, their fears inspired the concept of judicial control. But in this way diversity and pluralism reappeared once again. The physiocrats were in a tough spot, driven in contradictory directions. They needed a despot as well as a judicial body to control it; diversity led to unity which in turn meant the need for multiplicity. Ironically, judicial organizations (like *parlements*) were part of the old corporate society.

The doctrine of a unified sovereign was crucial as a revolutionary instrument, but it was questionable whether it could be compatible with the permanent attainment of liberty. There was danger of arbitrary power in unity since so potent a state had to be troublesome. The physiocrats confronted the ultimate dilemma of whether absolutism is the ally of freedom once liberty has been attained. Concentrated power alone could dissolve the old society; but the means of liberation can become a new leviathan and a threat to freedom.

The American concept of judicial control was a counterpart matching the proposal of the physiocrats. But physiocratic doctrine had little influence in the United States; Anglo-American constitutional development and a different set of historical sources led to the growth of the Supreme Court. The notion of judicial review flowered in America but failed in France. A powerful and independent judiciary was accepted in America, where it did not conflict with the need of absolute sovereignty to destroy the old corporate society. For in America, without a feudal past, the social revolutionary task was absent.

As in the case of Voltaire and the issue of religious toleration, the physiocratic definition of individual freedom entailed seeing liberty as the absence of restraint. Man was not to be coerced; the grounds of freedom were natural law. Nature was used normatively as a definition of right. At the same time the physiocrats thought they could derive natural rights from an empirical social order. They introduced the concept of a natural economic order, empirically defined, as the basis for these rights and freedoms.

But where was the evidence for their contention, since no such supposedly natural economic order of unrestrained individual freedom has ever existed? Throughout history economic life has had a coercive context, as with the guilds. An effort to discover empirical uniformity in economic development would have disclosed this inevitable aspect of control. Had the physiocrats been thoroughgoing empiricists, they would have discovered a natural order of coercion. This need not have made them conservatives. Facing up to economic realities does not mean they would have been made to believe any less ardently in individual liberty and freedom from restrictions, just as the empirical discovery that myths have existed need not have left Voltaire less devoted to the ethical ideal of intellectual freedom. Empiricism should have posed the problem of how to achieve the value of freedom: the issue of engineering the ideal of liberty in this persistent drift of coercion.

The physiocrats perceived that their natural economic order did not realistically exist. It was, they held, a tendency immanent in economic evolution. They introduced the idea of nature in normative terms to escape the implementation of values in the existential world. They called their ideal real by means of this notion of immanence.

But instead of there being an order of economic liberty built into economic development, one finds in modern history an expansion of organizational coercion. The physiocrats thought that there ought to be a tendency for economic coercion to wither; yet in the eighteenth century new economic changes were increasing coercion. The factory system meant a more disciplined economy than the guilds, an assertion of a new kind of coercion for an older version, as demonstrated by the silk workers' strikes in Lyons. Large-scale farms also imposed intensified controls over the workers. New coercions were bringing fresh problems in terms of the ideal of freedom. In economic terms there was more freedom within corporate society than under capitalism. The guilds, to be sure, involved real coercions, but factories entailed a system of even greater discipline.

The physiocrats took flight to the normative realm when the problem was an empirical one. Turgot thought that once the guilds were smashed, individual freedom in the labor field was assured. The new economic coercions of factories were not discussed. Du Pont speaks in terms of a world of free individuals. The physiocrats proposed to smash guilds to produce economic liberty, but the coercive content of new institutions, even of a so-called free market, was completely ignored. Under these fresh conditions of free contract coercion was to be freely elected, as if actual freedom had been achieved and the individual had a free choice. In the nineteenth century the question again arises of the choice of discipline; you get the job you can, but still you must accept the coercive context.

The physiocrats confused the normative and empirical ideas of nature. They evaded trouble by stating their norm as if it were already a fact, and avoided the empirical task of engineering into the real world their ideal of individual liberty. By virtue of the concept of immanence they reasoned a portion of social reality out of existence. "Immanence" only logically eliminated the new coercions, as if the idea of liberty could be automatically achieved. Voltaire too thought about intellectual freedom in a social void, apart from the coercions of a myth-bound culture; by means of the natural law concept the physiocrats conceived economic freedom in a social vacuum, independently of the coercions of the economic structure. They reasoned social facts out of existence, and harnessed the idea of economic liberty to a social void.

It is possible to use "nature" to identify a value with a fact, and eliminate the tension between them. It is an apparently happy way of life. But the gap between norm and fact makes people move, and gives them the problem of living. It was utopian to say that economic liberty was "immanent" in history. Nothing would need to be done, since the ideal was already embedded in reality. To see the norm of economic liberty in contradiction to history might be the beginning of how to bring the value into being. The eighteenth-century assertion of the ideals of intellectual and economic freedom were not only associated with social emptiness but helped to create it.

Like Voltaire the physiocrats had three possibilities. They could accept society and work within it; but these men pleaded not for more economic freedom but rather for economic liberty in all areas. The radicalism of their demand for economic liberty parallelled Voltaire's proposal for intellectual freedom. As an alternative approach the physiocrats could have substituted a new view of society. They did talk about the creation of a fresh social world; but they thought that once the old corporate order was abolished economic liberty would automatically come into being. They did not advance a new theory of society, but talked instead of a multiplicity of individualistic free atoms. They therefore did not have to investigate the coercion of, say, a silk factory, but could instead present a fluid social world in which individuals were of a Lockian type.

Essentially the physiocrats chose to follow a third option—trying to do away with the old society while presenting a scheme which had reference to no society. They advanced a conception of liberty which involved the reasoning away of society, the elimination of the social problem itself. The liberal norm was identified with empirical reality. As Voltaire did not explore intellectual freedom in a religious society, the physiocrats failed to investigate how to implement economic liberty in the real world.

These philosophes developed a sociological chasm which ultimately became the center of their theory. How to get liberty on a farm or a factory is a real question. It is in the nature of an ideal to judge the empirical world, which is why it is important to recognize the tension between a value and a fact. The real historical payoff came in the negation of the Enlightenment ideals; for when the gap got filled, during the conservative Reaction to the French Revolution, people said let us not have the ideals. There is a danger of the value going overboard when the fact is finally discovered.

4

Culture and Tradition: Condorcet

When the philosophes assailed the old order their ideals of freedom were devoid of an attempt to implement them. They did not associate the inherently myth-bound quality of life with their norms; instead they used moral abstractions to destroy the empirical world. And they defined natural law in terms of their utopian approach. The philosophes gave ideals an empirical reality at precisely the point empiricism was deserted; it gave them a sense of the real world even when it was being abandoned.

The eighteenth century has often been assailed as unhistorical. Carl Becker pointed out that considering the historical writings by Voltaire, Hume, and Edward Gibbon, this accusation against the era could hardly be justified. The philosophes were in fact conscious of the past; their critics simply do not like the Enlightenment treatment of history. That age did have a peculiar way of looking at history, for it perceived the past negatively. Both Voltaire and Diderot treated history as a mass of experience to which no special moral obligation was owed. (Locke had thought the earth belongs in usufruct to the living.) According to Voltaire and Diderot history was riddled with errors, and emancipation from it was optimally desirable; Holbach fought the Church, and Voltaire attacked the Middle Ages. This attitude of the philosophes was at odds with the wholesale historical involvement and devotion to tradition later in the nineteenth century, but was part of their special social position; they were rejecting the past as an aspect of their revolutionary role. History embraced the old corporate society they wanted to destroy: it was a receptacle for erroneous notions, the weight of the inertia of heritage.

The philosophes, even in their own terms of a drive for social change, had not taken an adequate view of history. The past can be viewed morally, as good or bad, or doctrinally, as right or wrong; but there is a realistic sense in which history must remain a social fact. Even though a radical intention might be morally desirable, still one must consider the problem of history as an empirical given. At any specific moment values and behavior patterns of the past are going to be vitally alive in all people to a greater or less extent; this is an empirical proposition. The philosophes themselves, even while they were revolting against their own society, were necessarily subordinate to the standards of the past. Historical norms remain relatively strong in our minds, which helps explain how tough societies are and why they cohere over time. The philosophes may have doubted and questioned the standards history imposed on them, but these were still massively present in French society of that day.

When the philosophes rejected history ethically they failed to confront the problem involved in trying to eliminate history as a social fact. Now all the philosophers of that age shared a concept of environmentalism: man was seen as a reflection of institutions. Hence thinkers like Condorcet, Turgot, and Condillac were confident that by altering social forms human nature could be changed. Locke's sensationalist psychology supported this approach, and it carried an enormous optimism with respect to abolishing history. Man was held to be untainted by Original Sin, a doctrine which had pinned social institutions to a static basis. Instead, human nature was seen as the product of outside society, which opened up infinite possibilities for social manipulation. Man's transformation then would require no internal development but only a change in the external culture. It is not surprising then that the philosophes exuded a great sense of social possibilities and creativity: it seemed that a new man could be created by new institutions.

Yet such an environmentalist outlook does not really touch the problem of history as a social fact. It can be conceded readily that social innovation will change the way people are.

But no one can ever start with a completely clean slate in time, a tabula rasa. Assuming the possibility of a raw humanity society would be infinitely malleable; still, people have to bear their historical inheritance. The problem with the environmentalism of the philosophes is that conceptually it denied the existence of history as an empirical given. Individuals are of course always touched by the outside world. The real problem of social change is that one must confront people who are already shaped by a preexisting environment, so it is only possible to inject as an influence a new environment which may be contradictory to the old one. At best one can erase and then write on the mind's slate; new things will usually get written over the old. It would be a fiction to define the situation with less complexity; otherwise the social fact of history would be evaded.

It is understandable that education played a prominent role in Enlightenment thinking; Condorcet expressed the age's demand for public schools. The physiocrats gave a mandate to the ideal sovereign: educate people so they are ready to accept the new social order. The philosophes characteristically wanted to remove education from the control of the Church. Here was another source of optimism; it is possible to concede how education might eliminate error and create a new human nature. But once again the point of view of the philosophes did not deal with the social fact of history. At best one education can be laid on top of another. An individual can be shifted from one school to a different one, which means that he must first unlearn and then learn anew. The issue becomes how much someone can successfully forget, which was not touched on in the Enlightenment's classical optimism. Despite the sense of creative power inspired by this direction of thinking in the philosophes, they had not confronted the real empirical problem.

An allied conviction was the Enlightenment's outlook on rationality: men are intrinsically reasonable, and if you advance sound ideas they will be accepted. In the face of abundant evidence that men now are not behaving rationally, the answer was that an implicit rationality must be liberated. This resolution constituted an avoidance of the problem, since it did not face up to the critical issue of emancipating people from the old tradition of error. The philosophes thought of individuals removed from culture, and then confronted by a new society.

An argument might be made that it is only in the transitional period that history as a social fact is important. But every transitional problem is really a permanent one. Difficulties of transition always shape the entire future: Marxian thought would later encounter the alleged transitional character of Stalin's Soviet Union. A conclusive case exists for thinking that the Enlightenment's sense of creative power arose from a clear evasion of the engineering problem involved in the dissolution of tradition. The philosophes were deficient in considering how to overcome what they considered erroneous and bad.

This is yet another instance of the mechanism of moral affirmation linked to empirical blindness. The idea of the past as an error was associated with avoiding the problem of manipulating the past out of existence. The same doctrinal aberration of flight from a factual problem recurs. Voltaire did not entertain questions about the necessity of theology, and the physiocrats evaded economic issues. The same characteristic technique, the use of natural law thinking, reasoned away history as a social fact.

Condorcet was the philosopher of the natural laws of the historical process. In sensing the applicability of the natural law formula to history, he repeated the same lack of realism as in the rest of Enlightenment thinking. Like the physiocrats, Condorcet discovered an immanent empirical world in history which corresponded to an ethical norm; brute facts thus simply would disappear. He proposed that an internal mechanism of history guaranteed the success of his ideals; it amounted to a theory of self-destruction on the part of history, the suggestion that a phenomenon contains within it a mechanism to force itself to disappear.

The idea of progress was a technical proposition allied to the notion of the continual disappearance of history. Through a process of growth and expansion history supposedly withered away; the new age was bound to appear, and old traditions doomed to dissolve. Turgot had proposed the idea that progress was taking place. And Condorcet developed the notion of progress in a natural law way; he was using it both as a norm and a fact, evading the living reality of history. But if you want to discover natural law in history, and succeed in understanding independent social forces, the approach to the past must not agree with the prevalent eighteenth-century outlooks.

Condorcet believed that certain natural laws of development proved that the Enlightenment antihistorical norm would triumph. His attitude toward the past was no longer one of contempt, because the past is in truth the matrix out of which the present and future flow. Various stages of development that he outlined fit together in such a way as to prove that progress was determined. Condorcet proposed that history contains the seeds of its own annihilation. Therefore it could not be all bad, since it included an impulse to dissolve in favor of something better. At the same time he studied history as if it were a storehouse of errors; yet he also believed that a contradictory impulse was triumphing over the past. He shared the antihistorical biases of the philosophes, but there was a tension in Condorcet that was not in other thinkers. He was at war with himself over his evaluation of history; he had to find in the past an instrument that overwhelmed itself.

According to the way Condorcet used natural law in historical development, tradition was eliminated and enlightenment substituted. One difficult problem remained however: retrogression. One might argue that it is impossible, a violation of the economy of nature, and that the purity of the natural scheme eliminated the issue. Progress would then be lineally upward. Condorcet says as much in the Introduction to his *Sketch for a Historical Picture.* If you accept retrogression as a possibility, it must be rationally fitted into the rest of the historical process; it can never be accidental. Retrogressive movement must be integrated into the larger frame of rationality and progress, as part of a pattern of a determined sequence; cycles of history are possible, but there can never be a sudden breakdown, for if retrogression is accidental then there can be no assurance about progress.

The eighteenth century viewed the past not as a simple line upward but in more complicated terms. The prevalent conception was that in ancient Greece and Rome things were pretty good; the medieval period was very bad; and in modern times everything was getting better. Yet this view entailed the problem of retrogression, and Condorcet could not logically avoid dealing with it. During his first five stages, from primitivity to Greece, development proceeded positively, straight upward. But in the sixth and seventh stages there was a sharp downward movement: "and now we have to confront the dark ages," he wrote, admitting a retrogression. It was a blatant contradiction to his Introduction.

Condorcet failed to integrate retrogression logically into a larger scheme; it just seems to happen. Priests and kings arose, causing all sorts of trouble. Why then can they not just reappear in even a twentieth stage? Condorcet's eighth stage restored the onward progress of history, but there has to be some assurance that there will not be another lapse. Condorcet did not deal with these questions; his theory had an extraordinary looseness to it, for his book was written at a white heat. He was fitting the contemporary prejudices of his century about history into the natural law mechanism. The general approach of transforming a norm into a fact and thus avoiding the implementation of value into reality was accomplished here. He was using the Enlightenment tactic of empirical evasion.

The social fact of history was dodged by Condorcet's approach; the belief in progress was a means for evading the empirical force of tradition. (Marxism would later on do the same.) According to the view of the philosophes, history was bad and its abolition good. But the real end of history could only be accomplished by a serious inquiry into social fact. By means of unlearning and reeducating, forgetfulness of history and tradition might be expected to yield a new society. In taking together the realms of religion, economics, and now history, it is apparent how different the political theory of the eighteenth century could have been. Serious inquiry might have taken place into how religion works, economics functions, and tradition grips. But instead of exploring the ways norms could be implemented we find a repetition of the natural law procedure of thinking.

In the three contexts of religion, economics, and history, we have found the same problem posed: the attempt to dissolve corporate society by means of the affirmation of norms. Once society was reasoned away by the invocation of the concept of nature, we do not find complete social emptiness in Enlightenment thought. Two things remain: a common sovereign, and a tenuous web of rationality holding society together. The philosophes had eliminated the forces of religion, economics, and tradition. But individuals could still be supposed to live as rationalistic atoms confronting the monarch. Helvetius's thought symbolizes the view of human beings as atomistic and manipulated. They would be without society and yet behave reasonably. Why did the Enlightenment retain this reliance on rationality? Once given the natural law principle they did not give it up.

If one eliminates the rational connections between men, taking away that which enables them to behave decently, life might become barbarous. The retention of rationality meant that thinkers could desocialize the individual and yet expect people to remain civilized. The philosophes could thereby eliminate society without needing to be afraid of the people. The web of rationality was a crucial weapon in reasoning away the rest of society. For if human irrationality begins to reappear, society also must come back; once one man takes advantage of another, there is coercion. Irrationality is the genesis of society. Therefore the Enlightenment had to maintain the element of rationality as a necessary remnant for the elimination of the rest of the social world.

The existence of a sovereign and isolated rational individuals was conceptually interrelated. It was the same fundamental image of Hobbes and Locke, and of all previous liberal reforming thought that invoked the concept of the state of nature— men without history and capable of being perfectly rational. What we have been discussing represents not a peculiarly French moment, but part of a pattern extending to the seventeenth century in England. The liberals sought to unravel man almost completely out of society. In trying to destroy the old corporate order, why should they have weighed down their theories with other considerations? It was an inevitable tendency of revolutionary theories. But it is not a necessary character of a thinker to be removed from the real world. These writers had the choice of abolishing an old myth, or creating a new one that would be flexible enough to retain liberty. But they opted instead for a path of evasion. The reasoning away of society was typical of what liberalism did everywhere in the seventeenth and eighteenth centuries. But when the Reaction against the Enlightenment set in, we will find an excess of empiricism.

5

Jean-Jacques Rousseau

The philosophes had advanced a theory of freedom which was dissociated from its implementation. By means of their use of natural law they reasoned out the content of any social order from the perspectives of political analysis. Still left intact were both a common sovereign and a thin web of rationality holding atom-like individuals together. These two social remnants were crucial in eliminating the rest of society; for in a truly disordered animal-like situation, a chaotic relationship of beings would create the kind of conflict that would reintroduce the necessity of society and its hierarchies. The implicit retention of sociability by the philosophes was a technique for obliterating the rest of society. The individual had been presented as a rational human being while the sociological necessities of myth, economic coercion, and history were omitted. It was a safe theory so long as someone did not question that some society still remained built into the premises of their thinking.

Rousseau, who had a complicated relationship with the mainstream of the Enlightenment, raised precisely this embarrassing question. In his "Discourse on the Origin of Inequality" he wrote: "philosophers who have inquired into the foundations of society, have all felt the necessity of going back to a state of nature; but not one of them has ever gotten there." He touched on exactly the mechanism by which previously a shred of sociability had been maintained in order to destroy the rest of society. He was telling the philosophes, as well as Locke, that they had not truly conceived of man in a state of nature. Rousseau destroyed the fairy tale by which it could be thought that human beings might exist as savages in the wilderness, for it was implied rationality that held them together. Rousseau wanted to eliminate the device by which social order gets wiped away. With him the Enlightenment's massive attack on the old society achieved its culmination; his own natural man was nonsocial, and conceived completely outside society.

The philosophes were horrified at Rousseau's completion of their work. Voltaire thought that Rousseau had presented an intolerable image of man. But Voltaire, in the course of his own attack on religion, had himself eliminated a major portion of the normal social connections between people. Rousseau was in fact fulfilling the logical implications of Enlightenment thinking. Voltaire's reaction to Rousseau illustrates how high a value had been placed on the special mechanism by which the social order was to be destroyed by subterfuge. Rousseau's ideas did not fit into Voltaire's vision of society, yet Rousseau's completion of eighteenth-century social thinking represented an internal imperative implicit in that century's whole line of thought.

Once man has been completely yanked out of the context of a social order the true functions of society stand out. Rousseau's confrontation with the possibility of a barbarian condition compelled a reversal of the whole process of eighteenth-century thinking. After society has been conceptually eliminated the intolerability of such a situation becomes apparent, and it is necessary to reconsider the virtues of the social order. No civilized person could accept the notion of barbarism. Rousseau's point, about no thinker having really gotten back to the state of nature, evoked a yearning for the old France, a need to adopt a constructive orientation to society. The only alternative to a more positive outlook on social order was to advance the savage ideal as a permanent one, which Rousseau did not do.

Rousseau started the counterrevolution against the eighteenth century which was to be the culmination of Enlightenment thinking. He recognized that compared to the hypothetical natural man the structure of a social order has to be shot through and through with coercion. He also saw that this coercive structure is desirable. Society transforms man from being a savage to a civilized creature. Rousseau was a defender

of the coercions inevitable in society. He assailed the philosophes, including the physiocrats and Voltaire; he saw the
necessary uses of the social order. Rousseau criticized those
who sought to desocialize the human being and reduce him to a
state of nature.

According to Rousseau's *Social Contract,* man is born free but
is everywhere in chains. He accepts that these chains are inevitable; he does not ask how to break them. Instead he inquires
into what can make these restraints legitimate; he was asking
about the best form of social coercion. He was therefore engaging in the reconstruction of society. It was the legitimacy of the
chains that intrigued him, how to go about getting the best
chains. First he restored society with its coercions, and then
posed the logical query, how can we make them legitimate and
ethically tolerable?

If Rousseau had stopped at this point he would have been a
profound conservative. He did attack atheists, he opposed the
atomism of the physiocrats, and he restored the inevitability of
society to his age. In fact he was to have a deep influence later
on reactionary theorists; Louis de Bonald and Joseph de
Maistre relied on him as much as the Jacobins did. But Rousseau was no conservative; his *Emile* shows how intensely he
hated the old corporate structure. For him the way out of the
dilemma was to examine the legitimacy of the necessary and
desirable coercions of society. He proposed to transform the
controls from a feudal to a nonfeudal form; he wanted constructively to reconstitute the quality of the coercions. In contrast,
the conservatives following his path restored the old society
and came back to defend the ancien régime. Rousseau did not
arrive at that destination, but instead invoked as an acceptable
image the eighteenth-century liberal vision.

Rousseau was at the same time half in and half out of the
eighteenth century. He was an opponent of the Enlightenment
who also shared its prejudices; the egalitarian and libertarian
principles of the eighteenth century were also his own. In their
attack on the old feudal system, and in the search for a unified
authority, the philosophes had maintained that the only legitimate source of coercion is the single sovereign. Rousseau
instinctively accepted characteristic eighteenth-century values.

The Enlightenment had reaffirmed a search for a single source of coercion which became traditional in liberal thought. The power of the state was limited because it operated in a coercionless void. But if the sovereign is the only legitimate source of coercion, and if, as Rousseau saw, society is in fact filled with coercion, then society becomes the one coercive civilizing force. The sovereign becomes coextensive with society. According to Rousseau's version of the social contract, the individual gives up everything when he enters society. Rousseau restored the coercion of society while retaining a unitary sovereign power; he identified sovereignty with society while holding that the only legitimate source of coercion can lie with the state. If man is everywhere in chains, then the state must spread itself over those chains to make them ethically acceptable. State power extends itself until every aspect of man's social life is touched. Rousseau therefore made the state coterminous with society. (Hobbes was different. For him only the sovereign has power, while for Rousseau society is originally coercive.)

Rousseau has been accused of promoting totalitarianism. He did though he was not a totalitarian in any modern sense. But a thinker moves in the stream of history, and the wholeness and integrity of a theoretical system are at odds with the particular insights of a framework which history will extract. Human beings can therefore never succeed in imposing themselves undividedly on history. It is of course unjust to judge Rousseau in terms of that portion of his theory which the future found strategically useful. Yet we must relate a thinker to historical reality, for events are always ruthlessly twisting people.

Rousseau did not invent the ideal he was promoting; he was rediscovering the ancient Greek polis. The real secret of the totalitarian concept of the state presiding over the whole of society is to be found initially in Locke, Turgot, and Voltaire. In their attack on feudalism they erected the state into being the only legitimate source of coercion. When you apply that ideal in the real world the state must work its way everywhere. The individual is atomized and hence left at the state's mercy. From the point of view of today's liberalism, feudalism becomes the antithesis of totalitarianism. In truth it is liberalism that is the historical author of the totalitarian model. Feudalism is permanently opposed to totalitarianism with its unified form of control. Rousseau was correct, coercion was inevitable and inescapable. But his accepting the liberal premise about the state could lead to totalitarianism. After the corporate order has been smashed by the state, the state can then take over the corporate order's coercive functions, nationalizing them. We must reject Rousseau's solution to the inevitability of coercion by not linking it so directly to the premises of the liberals about the singular legitimacy of the state.

The question of the General Will arose in the course of Rousseau's search for a means of legitimizing coercion, once he accepted its existence; for he was a good democrat. He questioned the morality of any despot, as he asked what makes societal chains ethically valid. The sovereign was subjected to inquiry; all authority was challenged. This was a problem that had been poorly explored by the physiocrats. In their system the sovereign is legitimate if he lets economic life flow freely and unhampered, according to the laws of nature. They had in mind a passive monarchy. But monarchs in the eighteenth century attained power through hereditary succession. What has a king, a product of inheritance, to do with following the mandates of natural law or utility? Monarchical will derived its source from a traditionalistic basis as opposed to the requirements of nature. The philosopher was to be king in the Platonic state; but Plato chose his rulers on the basis of their enlightenment. It was doctrinal confusion for anyone in the eighteenth century to think that making the child of a previous king sovereign had anything to do with Plato's philosophy or intentions.

The middle class was relying on an instrument to destroy the corporate order that was itself a part of the traditionalist order, hence the ultimate failure of the monarchy. It had a customary basis; the defense of the corporate system was hereditary rule, which was also the monarchy's own legitimizing support. The middle class tried to use one element of the ancien régime to undermine the rest of it. In the end the monarchy failed to fulfill the hopes of the middle class; giving up the monarchy was a painful thing for them. After the French Revolution the whole corporate system becomes solid and united as the battle between the monarchy and aristocracy gets forgotten.

The middle class persisted in its reliance on monarchy out of its fear of the democratic mass. If not the monarchy, the weapon for change could not be the aristocracy, and the masses became the obvious social instrument. But Voltaire was afraid of them. After the Revolution started the middle class does unwillingly come to accept democracy. Rousseau, though, did not need to wait for the Jacobins. His own search for the legitimate basis for coercion impelled him to confront the question of monarchy at once, and he blasted the doctrinal confusion of his contemporaries.

Rousseau's answer was that the legitimacy of coercion lies in the will of the coerced. Sovereignty is taken away from the monarchy. He recognized that monarchy cannot perform the job of liquidating the corporate system. Yet at precisely the point he is out of the stream of the eighteenth century he is in it; for although he repudiated monarchical absolutism he accepted other key liberal principles. For the idea of unitary sovereignty remained Rousseau's conviction at the moment he democratized it.

Rousseau's concept of the General Will was an attempt to retain the idea of unity, or a common good, which was close to the notion of natural law. Where can one get a single will when a mass of people rule? For him there was a danger in plurality reminiscent of the old society. Rousseau described a duality between a particular will and a General Will. When an individual is in the grip of his lower self, he will not see the common good. He will attend to the common good only when the rational will triumphs in him; freedom can take place if the rational will is in the ascendancy. Rousseau was working in a strain of thought that extends from Plato to Immanuel Kant. For Rousseau it was critical that unity be retained, since to his mind plurality meant a loss of rationality. It was even the task of the sovereign, as he saw it, to impose unity. Rousseau wrote about "forcing" man to be free, and to be made at one with himself. Pluralism can exist only when there is defection from the common good, the rational will. In Rousseau's thinking the concept of the General Will was the means by which freedom as well as unity could be achieved.

Rousseau's idea would seem to add up to sowing the seeds of totalitarianism. He did think that the General Will cannot really harm anyone, and that not even a single individual can be sacrificed for the public good. But he stressed the possibility of a new sovereign, apart from the people. Such a sovereign group can contend that it stands for the real rational will, which others do not see. In his system those who claim to represent the General Will are given unlimited power; they can coerce others, liberate them, forcing their rational wills to triumph. The Committee of Public Safety, soon to be formed, had its rationale. We are all basically at one, although some of us may unfortunately not perceive our brotherhood.

Political power had become a more devastating thing now. The authority of rulers was rationalized in different terms, unconnected with the old order. The feudal monarch also had been separate from the mass of the people but was linked to them by a decentralized chain. Rousseau proposes that when a mass rules itself, if you are coerced then you are being forced by yourself, by a power internal to you. In uniting the ideal of democracy with the insight into the pervasiveness of coercion, Rousseau proposed to muster an altogether new kind of accumulated power. Napoleon would smash the old society better than the monarchs could who were part of it. In Rousseau's terms, coercion becomes coterminous with society and is legitimized by democracy. When you fight such democratized coercion, you are really struggling against yourself. In the transition from the corporate world to liberalism, and then to Rousseau's thought, the amount of available political energy had been maximized.

Rousseau's discovery of the pervasiveness of coercion led to its nationalization through the utilization of the state as the only legitimate means of coercion. This is how to understand Rousseau's concept of the General Will. There were many mitigating forces within his theory; he was trying to absorb a new insight within an old technique, and he wanted to retain liberal ideas in the face of his fresh perception. He thought he had restored the significance of coercion within a liberal framework. As we shall see, however, society will bounce back powerfully when it demands full compensation after its arrogant treatment by the philosophes.

6

Rousseau and Our Constructive Problem

Rousseau had seized on his insight into the fact of social life and the inevitability of coercion; using the preconceptions of the philosophes about a unitary sovereign and the state being the only legitimate source of coercion, he produced the image of a totalitarian state. According to his notion the power of the state becomes coextensive with the social order. Rousseau's contribution gets dramatized in the light of the philosophes having earlier eliminated from their social theory myth, economic restraints, and history.

The issue of religion in Rousseau was critically important, and the chapter on "Civil Religion" in his *Social Contract* is famous. Much can be found there that is harmonious with the ideals of Voltaire; the attack on intolerance, clerical fanaticism, and revelation were characteristic of other eighteenth-century thinkers. Yet the surface iconoclasm and skepticism in Rousseau is misleading. His criticism of Christianity is specific; most importantly to him it undermines the civic sense of obligation. It is too otherworldly, and does not elicit the loyal qualities of military virtue required by the state. Rousseau thought that the obligations of citizenship are of this world; he was under the influence of Machiavelli, as he used the same argument and shared the identical worship of classical civilization. Rousseau proposed a humanistic, secular civic religion. He also criticized the idea that man should be under the allegiance of both the Church and the state, since two such masters meant to him that the proper bond to the state could be undermined by the claims of the Church.

Rousseau was thinking constructively of the uses of religion; he saw the significance of a myth as inevitable and necessary. He knew that no state has ever been founded without a religious basis and that myth is a unifying force in society. Rousseau had another religion besides Christianity: citizenship. He carried forward the abstract recognition of the permanence of social order in the specific context of religion. He was inquiring into which religion is best since we live in a world where the religious element in society is inevitable. At one and the same time he hated the Church but acknowledged the inevitability of a religious role.

In his discussion of civil religion he was not thinking about the possibility of a separate body within the community but of a state religion. If the state is the only legitimate source of coercion, and religion is a permanent fact, then a state religion becomes the logical conclusion. What then becomes of the intolerance and fanaticism he had attacked? He was proposing a religion of civic duties and rights to take the place of old religion. But betrayal remains a serious matter. Rousseau held that anyone who violated civil religion deserves severe punishment; he proposed banishment and death for such offenses. Although he might seem to have forgotten his old criticisms of intolerance, he was reinstituting fanaticism and legitimizing it through secularization. Once intolerance was nationalized in the hands of the state sovereign it was moral, and therefore he could chillingly insist that it was impossible to live with "the damned."

Robespierre was a just disciple of Rousseau. The integrity and wholeness of any social philosopher does contrast with the historical movements that pillage a thinker. No simple equation can ever be set up between a writer's unique effort and the uses to which his ideas get put. Alfred Cobban has argued that the chapter on civil religion represents an unfortunate lapse on Rousseau's part, but this point of view misses the whole logic of the process of which Rousseau was a part.

Rousseau was articulating a principle deeply embedded in the whole social movement of his age. The concept of the state as the sole legitimate source of coercion, added to the recognition of the necessity of social order, yielded Rousseau's notion of civil religion. The revolutionaries instituted severe punishments, attacked the Church, and were intolerant in trying fanatically to enforce civil religion; there was as little freedom in their state as in the old one. Both Rousseau and the Jacobins were in the grip of certain developmental forces which cannot easily have been avoided.

Would Voltaire have been horrified at the new fanatics? If you contrast Voltaire's views on religion with either Rousseau's civil religion or with what the Jacobins did, he had only himself to reproach, for he avoided implementing liberty into a situation that required some mythical basis for the state. He could have provided a formula for salvaging real freedom. The arrival of the civil religion of the Jacobins represented the vengeance of the social fact of religion on the philosophes for their irresponsibility in eliminating it. Here you have to divorce any element of guilt or blame; the omission of one thinker was capitalized on by another as the ideal went down the drain.

Rousseau only vaguely spelled out the content of his civil religion; the whole tenor of his *Social Contract* was abstract and universal. Yet he wrote that the size of the state should be limited. The tie of solidarity diminishes with the territorial extent over which it is extended. In stating that human beings share certain universalistic characteristics, he was reflecting the great cosmopolitanism of the eighteenth century; it had an image of a universal world, the unity of mankind. Therefore when he made a myth he included all of humanity. Yet the sense of community diminishes with its extent, and he knew about the need for solidarity.

Rousseau sensed that if political theory must include religion, universalism will provide an obstacle to the sense of community. He found the solution to his dilemma in nationalism as a means of holding societies together; hence his special interest in Poland and Corsica. A sense of national separateness became the substance of his civil religion.

According to Rousseau a nation should stick to its traditions, and find in them a political center around which emotions can gather; he was giving depth to a political theory because he was aware of the power of religion. He chose to get away from abstract cosmopolitanism to arrive at a more provincial concept. To have cohesion there is a need for a sense of continuity with a distinctive past. He wanted to celebrate national traditions; nationalism, an effective form of civil religion, would come from the customs of a country. The task of the legislator in Rousseau's view was to dig up and foster those elements of the past that unite the people in nationalistic terms. He wanted to create a civil religion through the technique of nationalism, which is a phenomenon peculiarly reliant on history.

Here the social fact of history was coming back; tradition, like religion, reappears. Rousseau can be balanced with Condorcet. It was precisely the power of the past that the philosophes wanted to get away from. Tradition was in some sense the embodiment of the whole ancien régime. The Enlightenment thinkers had thought that by linking themselves to history, and the bondages of the past, they would be tied to the old corporate order.

Rousseau solved this problem by exploiting the principle he had inherited. If you are to have any traditions they can stem from only one legitimate fountain: the nation. In glorifying *La Patrie* custom got nationalized just as religion was, too. He united the perception of the inevitable force of history with the old liberal notion that coercions, to be legitimate, must stem from the state. His approach was not cooked up out of his imaginative power alone. These abstract alternatives were also involved in the history of the period, and in some sense Rousseau was reflecting them. Robespierre tried to build a religion of humanity, which could not survive until it became French nationalism and a myth of the Revolution. With the Jacobins and Robespierre *La Patrie* swallowed up the abstractions of the Enlightenment; the idea of the French people became a nationalistic symbol divorced from any cosmopolitanism, and supported the exploitation of other peoples by Napoleon.

The preconceptions of Rousseau were those of the philosophes of his period. The state was held to be the only legitimate source of coercion; at the same time unified power had been linked to a social vacuum, an atomistic harmony. Rousseau retained the idea of unity, but the conception of the state as the only legitimate source of coercion is plausible only so long as the rest of the social fictions of the philosophes are retained. Once society is restored, Rousseau's notion of a civil religion, and of a civil history, results in an inevitable trend toward a totalitarian effect.

We are confronted with the task of rebuilding the theory of the philosophes, restoring the social facts as well as erecting new principles of legitimate authority. For us to implement the ideals of the Enlightenment two corrections are now necessary: we must accept the force of Rousseau's attack on social atomism, and at the same time eliminate the central premise of unified sovereignty. In revising the theory of liberalism these two operations must go together. As part of the Enlightenment's attack on the decaying feudal system, atomism and a unified sovereign went together; but both propositions must be reexamined. It is probably safe to assume that we all accept the basic Enlightenment ideal of universal freedom.

Modern totalitarianism would be logically impossible without the prior development of the liberal movement. Feudal decentralization, as well as the French liberal image of the eighteenth century, help to explain the genesis of Rousseau's ideas. It would be inconceivable to derive Rousseau from Sir Robert Filmer, that philosophic spokesman for the old social order. For in the ancien régime the modern state does not exist nor does the concept of sovereignty. The principle of unity followed from the liberal image of the philosophes.

It makes good sense that the dominance of the image of the Greek polis was so striking for Rousseau. He did not believe in representation but put his trust in the small city-state. Other thinkers, such as Machiavelli, James Harrington, and Montesquieu, had also admired the Greek polis. What can account for this peculiar quest for the polis, and how does it shed light on our larger problem? As these writers romanticized the polis it was an all-embracing entity, a community in which there was no distinction between state and society. Beginning with the Renaissance the small city-state stands as the absolute negation of the divided, decentralized authority of the medieval corporate society.

In this idealized conception the polis not only represented unity, but also became the home of individual freedom. The correspondence between individual freedom and community was made possible by the notion of a preponderant degree of civic participation. The capacity of everyone to participate in the manifold spheres of the state would provide a certain freedom; yet there could be no rights whatever. The power to participate does create a quality of freedom. The polis embodied an equivalence of state and society that underlay its definition of freedom. Rousseau was really a supreme individualist, and also a collectivist; in the ideal of the city-state he found a way of establishing an identity between individual freedom and collective supremacy.

Rousseau repudiated monarchical sovereignty and the desire for negative liberty, finding his whole problem solved in the polis; he was legitimizing state coercion with democracy. The Greek ideal was the only available historical image; it might have been obsolete institutionally yet it solved other issues in the period. If the polis could have been made real Rousseau would have had a solution to his general problem. Liberty was to be defined in terms of participation and not in connection with rights. The polis was attractive to Rousseau in that it made the state and society coterminous.

Reconstructing Athens in the eighteenth century was, however, completely impossible. First of all, the polis had a slave base for its society which permitted such mass participation as did take place; citizens cannot participate full-time unless they are free of other work. Secondly, the polis was small; but modern history has meant an institutional drift to large states, and sheer size means the passivity of citizens, as opposed to the activity possible in antiquity. Thirdly, the modern state is so complicated that no one can see the whole of it except in shadowy outline; this irreducible pluralism is at odds with the ancient Greek ideal of the small, simple polity.

Modern man's life must be pluralistic, and therefore the state can be only one of his preoccupations. Democratic theory must recognize all these changes, and the degree of inherent quiescence which is involved in modern citizenship. The intense activity of Greek citizens is now impossible, and to a large extent passivity has become necessary. If you want participation under our modern conditions, often only essentially symbolic activity is possible; the totalitarian states have known about how to force participation through such means as the empty raising of hands.

The futile search for the polis, the impossibility of recapturing its participation and solidarity, highlights the whole problem. Given the failure of such an entity to arise, the idea of a unitary sovereign must be given up, if the attempt is to be made to engineer liberty in society. Since the polis is impossible in modern life the whole definition of politics and society has to be revised.

Our central theoretical problem will be, what in fact is a free society, and what is the role of the state in its attainment? What kind of state should be established? The preconceptions of the Enlightenment and Rousseau's own image were bound together. But the ideals of the philosophes were combined with a social vacuum, leading to the later shattering of their norms through an emphasis on the social order, which is what the Reaction amounted to. We will try to define freedom in terms of a real society and still escape the solidaristic outcome of Rousseau. Or if we accept the necessity of social coercion, must we arrive at Rousseau's conclusions? As we shall see, these alternatives do not exhaust the possibilities of the implementation of liberty.

The problem of the relation of the free state to achieving a free society was not the issue of that age. By the criterion of historical victory and defeat problems have to be solved in order for people to survive. But the liberals succeeded in defeating their opponents. All their errors—the individual as an isolated atom, the false conception of unity—did not prevent the French Revolution or the rise of the middle class.

The Enlightenment succeeded in history in spite of its mistakes. Our own central preoccupation (that is, the role of the state in attaining a free society) comes from the twentieth century; it is the issue of current politics, connected with matters that arose after the end of the eighteenth century: how do we implement the ideal of freedom in a socially coercive world? (Or perhaps the central issue should be defined in terms of the decline in faith, the substitution of rationalism for theological speculation, which would lend an entirely different perspective to eighteenth-century thought.)

One might wonder whether there is an anarchy of possible interpretations. Can we understand a past era in terms of our own preconceptions, and is any such interpretation as good as any other? Interpretive relativity does exist up to a point. But whereas approaches differ because of their theoretical point of origin, the facts need not be in dispute. Let us put aside for the moment the basic problem of how to define what a fact is. Two interpretations need not contradict one another if they are built on the same empirical basis. We are not reduced to the subjectivistic conclusion that any viewpoint is as good as any other. Interpretations are capable of checking one another, and factual data do threaten certain possible outlooks.

There is nonetheless an arbitrary element in our making central the problem of the state in promoting a free society. Although the issue is one whose solution did not then determine historical success or failure, it is the problem of our own century. At some time between the eighteenth and the twentieth centuries it becomes the realistic problem. At a certain point the issue will enter the arena of history, and determine the outcome of the struggle. We are going through history to reconsider the preconceptions that were critical when people considered the problem of personal freedom and state control, for we have to know why people cherish the prejudices they still retain.

Part II

REACTION AND AUTHORITARIANISM

7

The Setting

The atomistic society of Enlightenment thinking contrasted with Rousseau's solidaristic outlook. Yet the conceptions of the philosophes and Rousseau represented the same passion for unity and the identical conviction about the state as the source of legitimacy for coercive authority.

Once the Reaction set in against the Enlightenment and its Revolution, the historical setting involved in our analysis presents diverse social systems. Different implications existed within each of the several societies and therefore our geographic area has to broaden. The French Revolution was a European phenomenon, so we must deal with England and Germany as well as France. The issue is how to find a common movement of ideas in such a diversity of institutions and environments.

From an economic viewpoint England was, by the early nineteenth century, in the full tide of the Industrial Revolution, which began in the mid-eighteenth century. Germany had been scarcely touched by commercial and industrial enterprise, and remained mostly attached to agriculture; capital was frozen in land. The effect of the Napoleonic wars meant a draining away of more capital for imports (Werner Sombart thought Germany was less advanced economically in 1830 than 1802). In France the drive for industrial development was midway between Germany and England, and marked by extreme economic diversity.

In the political context a series of remarkable variations could also be found. England came out of the Napoleonic period with a long tradition of national unity and constitutionalism; it had an idea of organic community that was expressed by writers like Richard Hooker and Edmund Burke. In France Louis XVIII sought to negotiate a new system, a half-breed between the ancien régime and the Revolution; that country was in a situation of deep and ultimate conflict, for although it had national unity there was an absence of community. Radical democrats still fought against the absolutism of corporatism. In Germany, however, nationhood had not yet been achieved, and thirty independent principalities existed; 1848 would raise the question of unification, which itself overrode traditional questions of political theory.

From the point of view of intellectual history a comparative national approach is also necessary. In England the principles of the constitutional settlement of 1688 were those of Locke and were broadly shared. France, however, had a sharp, irreconcilable conflict between the norms of a democratic trend and those of the ancien régime. In contrast, Germany was only at last awakening to new ideas and thoughts.

How can such different societies construct a common movement of thought known as the Reaction? A remarkable diversity in the rate of European development can be found. But the problem is not hopeless; the conservative ideas we will be talking about derived their impetus only secondarily from unique domestic societal influences, since its primary objective was negative. For what the Reaction arose against was the same everywhere: the Enlightenment and the Revolution. The common mood was negative and the shared target the Revolution. The French Revolution itself became an event of universal impact. Even on the institutional plane, with the anti-Napoleonic Holy Alliance, Europe could unite against the Revolution. The remarkable negativism of Metternich's ideas was held together by his antagonism to the ideals of the French eighteenth century.

In the world of intellect remarkable similarities can be evoked by a common enemy. Karl Mannheim held that in the life of the mind the latest antagonist determines the categories of argument. Nowadays communism lays down our own framework of debate. From the Americans for Democratic Action on the Left to the National Association of Manufacturers on the Right we find a reiteration of the same ideas in all these groups; diverse movements are united by a common drive against communism. Such a shared element, historically and intellectually, gives a similar point of departure for our analysis of the Reaction.

The diversity of national settings combined with the common object of the attack on the Revolution leaves us with the problem of understanding the integrity of a thinker's ideas in the context of history. For a specific national setting may link dynamism at home with conservatism abroad. For example, Burke in England was a liberal; yet when he spoke against the French Revolution he was a conservative. Therefore common conservatism may be linked to liberalism within a particular country. Burke illustrates how a unique English setting can have inspired liberalism; yet the French Revolution called forth conservatism. It is important to see that Burke was throughout being philosophically consistent. Hegel, too, had conservative and liberal ideas: in connection with national unification he was a liberal, yet his conservatism stands as one of the high points of the Reaction.

Burke held that the French Revolution was an expression of an international revolutionary movement. The Revolution had initially appealed to the same groups in different countries, and they can be lumped together in the category of the bourgeoisie. But the middle class enthusiasm for the Revolution was limited; after it had attained some reforms, the French bourgeois became frightened and tired. The French middle class supported Napoleon and the restoration of Louis XVIII, but not Charles X. In England, too, the bourgeoisie became terrified; figures like Charles James Fox and Richard Sheridan were thoroughly discredited, and the middle class enthusiasm for the Revolution waned sharply with the coming of the Reign of Terror.

The forces most bitterly opposed to the Revolution produced the Reaction; it did not arise from a fatigued or disenchanted bourgeoisie. The Church, the aristocracy, and the landed gentry banded together; the articulation of the Reaction came from the extreme Right. In a revolutionary situation the oscillations of opinion are bound to be tremendous: consider the views of Richard Price as opposed to the Duke of Wellington, or Robespierre in contrast to Louis de Bonald, as examples of how intellectual forces were polarized. The extreme political positions became the sources of the arguments expressed. In the twentieth century the Bolshevik Revolution pitted America against Russia in much the same way that England stood to France at the end of the eighteenth century. Our right-wing Republicans expound anticommunism, and much the same thing happened in England then. Prior to the Tory Reaction England had had a powerful liberal movement; but the conflict with the Revolution produced the Earl of Eldon and the Reaction, which meant a reversion to the defense of every privilege as sacred. Any reform could seem like a step to revolution; the events after 1789 in France crushed the liberal forces in England. The Right took over leadership in this conflict, as the political forces became polarized.

The theory of the Reaction then came from the monarchy, the clergy, and the nobility; the supporters of these groups expressed its philosophy. It was an interesting and novel alliance, since in the eighteenth century the monarchy had fought both the Church and the aristocracy. The categories of the conflict then had meant that royal absolutism was pitted against the old corporate order. What had happened to unite them was a new alignment historically. In the course of the Revolution the middle class finally attacked the monarchy; it stood in the end under the banner of republicanism. With this desertion of the monarchy the political line-up was altered, as the middle class stood alone against the monarchy and the corporate order. The old groups now took their stand together. The historical battle that had existed since the end of the Middle Ages was over; the dualistic conflict between the forces for unification and change against those defending the decentralized ancien régime was obliterated by the French Revolution. Once a new enemy, in the form of bourgeois republicanism, threatened all of them, the issue was never again the same.

Ironically Louis XVIII was criticized by the nobility for not being strong enough and unwilling to assert the power of absolutism. The aristocracy finally realized its inner connection to the monarchy. The old feudal classes attained a new cohesion, forgetting their ancient struggles. The new republicanism was a menace to them all.

The reactionary alignment after a great social revolution produced a new combination of forces. The Revolution raised up a fresh struggle that made the old conflicts obsolete. It was not that an old battle had been fought to culmination but that another and more important struggle lay underneath the previous one. Had the feudal classes recognized their common enemy in time, they might have done better before the Revolution. But it took the Revolution to make the reactionary groups understand what they had in common, and this is characteristic of revolutions. If the political positions earlier had reflected actual social tensions, they might have been resolved within the old society; but the arguments had rung false, the bourgeoisie had been on the sidelines, and therefore a revolution had broken out.

The sociological position of the reactionary theorists, and the question of how philosophers came to these conservative groups and advanced a rational defense of their position, raises the issue of the nature of thought itself and its relation to political change. We must reflect on the thinking process; for thought is a systematizing experience that can never correspond to the full complexity of existence. Thought constructs ideal archetypes that cannot fit the ultimate irrationality of reality. Political theory is therefore in some sense always on the side of change and reform; as a rationalizing activity it is inevitably in conflict with the manifoldness of existence.

The true conservative is an unthinking man who is unconscious of the whole question of conservatism. He is someone who expresses by his own activity his commitment to the status quo. Thought therefore gets forced upon the conservatives who make up the ruling group and the Revolution makes thinking necessary for them. The conservative acts without reflecting; he is only shaken by the Revolution into asking questions about the good life. As Mannheim wrote, the Revolution dictates the categories of the Reaction. It means that the conservative must think and argue over what is involved; he must now defend himself rationally. His dilemma is that he has to reason about the undesirability of thought, which becomes a commonplace in conservative thinking.

Burke therefore attacks political metaphysicians; he reiterated that when people begin to think, everything is already lost. Thought itself appears to him as the great social disease. An inherent contradiction existed between the conservative mode of communication and its objective: conservatism was a rationalizing endeavor, even though that was the very object that conservative activity was trying to eliminate. Burke thought that metaphysicians were bad, but he had had to argue metaphysically. The problem was not solved until Hegel's own specific refutation of the Enlightenment.

8

Romanticism

The conservative hostility to abstractions and to the radical role of thought itself in politics and society provides a key to understanding romanticism and its relation to reactionary theory. William Wordsworth in England symbolizes the repudiation of systematic speculation. He proposed to embrace the infinite complexity of reality, which defies any rational system; his position was that of an instinctive ally of conservatism. Frederick Watkins has proposed that romanticism in politics was exclusively the property of reactionaries. But one has only to look at the Revolution itself, or at Rousseau, to see that for every reactionary romantic there is a revolutionary romantic. Romanticism then is not the exclusive property of any reactionary group.

Revolutionaries can accept a romantic theory. Revolution is of course necessarily weighted on the side of change, and therefore a natural ally of thought. But theorizing is more complicated than it might seem and has an aspect which is the reverse of its capacity to be abstract and challenging to reality. If thought is corrosive in that it systematizes, theorizing can also paralyze action. Thinking schematizes complexities, yet the implementation of ideas requires action. Thought is on the side of change in that it challenges the variety in reality but it also inhibits the translation of ideas into action because of the purity of ideal types. The revolutionary must translate into the raw world of action those notions that inspire change but do not correspond to reality. The stereotype of the intellectual is that of an unsettling fellow who yet can do nothing—a mere thinker.

A danger of radicalism does arise in any theoretical effort but paralysis comes when systematizing has to confront the translating of ideals into reality.

When revolutionary norms move into the realm of reality they become romantic. The implementation of ideals requires a departure from rationalism. By his own route the revolutionary adopts precisely that romantic mood of indeterminacy and complexity that gets defended in reactionary thought. In the world of action the Revolution and the Reaction meet; both the revolutionary and the conservative are justifiably distrustful of thought. Georges Sorel, a syndicalist revolutionary, can therefore be put alongside Burke. Sorel feared that people will only dream of radical achievement; he wanted them to act and reject thought, and he was an irrationalist frightened of systematic thinking as potentially crippling. Sorel therefore blasted abstractions as Burke did.

The problem of action united the revolutionary and the conservative in the realm of romanticism. The conservative wants to defend a pattern of activity, a preexisting standard of behavior. Thought can function as a component of action, but never at a long distance. The conservative seeks to defend current reality while the revolutionary wants to create a new world. Yet to the extent that both the revolutionary and conservative share an action element, in each case there is a romantic component.

A paradox arises in the Reaction's dualistic approach to the Revolution. The conservatives attack it as a work of metaphysicians and also assail it as the product of misplaced religiosity. Was the Revolution metaphysical or religious, the product of calculating men or mad fanatics? It was both, and that was the cause of the two criticisms. It was simultaneously the product of the Enlightenment and of romanticism. The dilemma of the revolutionary is to keep ideals alive in the real world of action; according to Marx the solution was to "act as men of thought and think as men of action." It is the only way to effect major social change, for when you go from the realm of thought to that of action there is a danger of becoming conservative because of the return to the world of complex reality.

Marx in the end, with Lenin's help, led to both Trotsky and

Josef Stalin. Soviet bureaucracy, on the other hand, stands for the reconstitution of conservatism within a revolutionary framework. Bureaucratic practice has its rationalistic side but there is a difference between the rationalizing spirit of natural law and the mood of the bureaucrat who enforces rules on every occasion. The purpose of the bureaucrat is to keep the system going. What Burke wanted was to keep customary activity traditional. The bureaucrat, too, fears unsettledness. Rationalism gets forced on the bureaucrat by conservative necessity. Romanticism, on the other hand, means a plunge into the real world; bureaucracy is the symbol of the victory of such a plunge. The bureaucrat aspires to become a Burkean type. Romanticism means a surrender to felt contingencies, and it was Burke who was a believer in compromise.

The bureaucrat is notoriously short-sighted, advocating accommodation to an unconquerable world. To him, for example, the existence of the necessity of six vouchers seems rational, while he does not examine the problem of why six vouchers should be necessary. One is left in legitimate doubt whether bureaucratic rationality is the ally of the Enlightenment or of conservatism.

In an attempt to get at the indefinable nature of action we arrive at an operational definition of romanticism. It is that mood which, in distinction to a faith in a rationally calculated universe, adapts itself to a situation in which all elements are not rational. Romanticism fits itself to contingency. In literature it stressed the unique and the irreducible as opposed to any system of rule-making that tries to make things uniform.

The problem of how conservatives and liberals can both be romantics should be understood in terms of how both movements shared a preoccupation with action. For action involves a desertion of the purely systematic since the world is never reducible to any philosophic structure. Romanticism insists that we recognize the contingent. In this spirit Burke was seeking to rationalize a system of traditionalized action; his opposition to reflection was indicative of a concern with action, which involves realms of experience that contradict reflection.

The Jacobins, following Rousseau, wanted to destroy Burke's old corporate world, yet they had to enter the world of action; therefore they had in their own way to become romantics and desert the spirit of Voltaire. The mood of the world of action distinguishes both the Jacobins and Burke from Voltaire.

What else can explain the fact that romanticism embraces both radicals and conservatives? The Revolution imposed its categories on the Reaction; and therefore reactionaries had to think and answer arguments. Any deterministic theory can eliminate the immediate quality of action yet still be involved in the problem of action. The mood involved in the introduction of any scheme is essentially different from the foundation of that system. Burke thought that the man of action is always making choices, and that statesmanship is an instinctive proposition. Actual political activity does involve an intuitive element. For Burke the experience of the aristocracy was an essential quality of leadership. A revolutionary confronts a similar matter in holding that a sense of the situation permits him to function and proceed; no such guide exists in any rational system. In terms of the problem of experience and reflection both revolutionaries and conservatives share a similar set of attitudes.

Social thought is necessarily unsettling, yet every social thinker does not have the inclination to implement his thoughts. A conservative, when he writes, is already partially lost for he has entered the realm of polemic and reasoning. If you answer an argument you make an issue out of something and expand the matter, although ignoring it is always an alternative. Yet there are times when you must reply to an opponent. A revolutionary by nature must begin with a blueprint, while a conservative is most at home entirely in the realm of behavior.

Rational prediction when applied to reality is never complete; a sense of the situation is needed, and therefore one must estimate, gamble, and guess. Political situations are charged with contingency, and Burke thought that the quality of statesmanship is to be able to meet this uncertainty. The Enlightenment in a sense produced both a conservative and a revolutionary offshoot, Burke and Robespierre. But it was Burke's expressed conviction, in contrast to eighteenth-century thinking, that in a world irreducible to system one must look to tradition, to supra-systemic norms, as a guide to conduct.

The Enlightenment thinkers had little practical experience of politics. Tocqueville pointed out the abstractness in their written works, and that their utopias were directly related to their inexperience. It has been argued that reactionary theorists, in contrast, had more political experience. But there is only superficial evidence to fortify this idea. It is true that Burke was a politician; and he saw a lot more than others on the nature of the operations of government. Yet the issue of practical experience does not in the end prove critically important. It did not mean that the Reaction had more understanding of the actual functioning of society. The Reaction did see a good deal that the philosophes missed, but the conservatives were still blind to the nature of revolution as a social fact.

It was not so true of Hegel but does remain accurate about the rest of the conservative writers; they saw the Revolution as merely a terrible event that had been created by rascals, a disastrous plot of evil men to be put down forever. As far as they were concerned, revolution was the end of all good things; no virtues or graces can survive it.

Every commentator has pointed out the insight of Burke and Maistre in predicting the coming of military dictatorship and ultimately the Restoration; yet neither of them hinted that the Revolution would repeat itself, and that the Restoration itself would disappear. The reactionary theorists failed to see the experience of the Revolution as a momentous fact in Western European history. The Revolution becomes for the conservatives a simple and artificial construct, just as the philosophes had missed the complexity of their existing social world; the philosophes thought they could reason away society while the reactionaries believed they could think away the Revolution as intellectualist. For Bonald no revolution was possible. This peculiar empirical blindness could be sustained because these reactionaries had no experience with the passions and dreams of the revolutionary period; in France many of them became exiles who associated only with each other, and developed an emigré mentality.

It is not then a question of the experience of the conservatives, or whether they had more or less of it, but rather an issue of what kind of experience they had known. They were alienated from the Revolution itself. There are different orders of experience; the revolutionary theorists were blinded to the perplexity of introducing ideals into reality, while the reactionaries lost contact with the possibility of an end to the Restoration. They were equally obtuse to the insurgent impulse of Revolution itself. But man's striving to build an ideal world, the problem of aspiration, is as much a fact as his submission to the status quo.

9

Edmund Burke

The interplay between unique national settings and a common negative reactionary impulse meant a more complicated picture in Britain than elsewhere. Enlightenment ideas, ever since Locke in the seventeenth century, had been a dominant part of the settled principles of British government. The arrangement of 1688 became an institutional tradition. Yet the British acceptance of the Enlightenment heritage since Locke, after the French Revolution, had to be mustered in an attack against the Enlightenment in France. Burke was, besides, as a leader in the Whig party a guardian of the 1688 Revolution, which only added to a paradoxical situation. Left-wing Whigs like Fox insisted on applying the principles of 1688 to the French Revolution.

Every past revolutionary situation gives to subsequent periods certain ideal principles which, if they are to be stabilized, must be bureaucratized and emasculated of their revolutionary meaning. A revolution, if successful, must eliminate from its ideals that quality that inspired the original upheaval. Therefore Martin Luther eventually had to repudiate anarchistic individualism, and the Reformation took its final form in Calvinism. In England alone is the chief problem of the Reaction that of stabilizing Enlightenment principles. In France and Germany there was outright confrontation. The task of implementing ideas differs from that of opposing them, and is more difficult than simply destroying a system of thought. Burke had to search for points within the Enlightenment that would eliminate revolutionary concepts: he always claimed to be a follower of Locke, and elements in Locke had to be found to use against that thinker's heritage, so that the outcome of Locke as it took shape in France did not have to be accepted in England.

Therefore Burke disagreed with the philosophes about the concept of freedom; he departs from Locke by arguing over who is a true liberal. In his "Letter" to a member of the National Assembly he argued that "men of intemperate minds cannot be free." Freedom was defined not as liberation from external forces but as emancipation from internal passions; the individual was to be freed, spiritually and psychologically, from himself. (Burke was appealing back to a tradition starting with the Greeks and which extended to Rousseau and Kant.)

Burke had established a link by which the old society could be justified in the name of freedom: the impact of society can prevent the individual from being under the domination of his passions. The organized coercive authority of the community gives the individual his freedom. Burke restored the old society by means of accommodating it to a theory of freedom. He identified freedom with social coercion instead of defining liberty in terms of detaching the individual from the external social order.

We can see here the enormous influence of Rousseau on the Reaction. While societies differ (and Rousseau's was not Burke's), the intellectual mechanism was the same in both cases. The social element had been restored and freedom redefined by means of the notion of a higher and lesser man. But Rousseau in his *Social Contract* called the higher self associated with society a rational will, and it was sometimes spelled out mathematically. It can be corrosive of existent reality; Kant knew that if we call higher purpose a rational one, it holds out a danger to the social order. To harness it to the status quo and rob this definition of social destructiveness, Burke devised a different meaning for the term rational; it clearly had a romantic nature. He used the concept of reason not in the Enlightenment sense, but instead interchangeably with the notions of feeling and prejudice. Reason was turned into its antithesis. Hence Burke can blast Rousseau as a political mathematician, since Rousseau didn't spell out the romantic implications.

According to Burke the emancipation of will from lower compulsion is accomplished by means of feeling and early childhood prejudice. In associating freedom with the old order it became defined as the pursuit of primitive channels of behavior that the individual has performed early on. The Enlightenment had linked its theories to a social void; in the Reaction, however, society is restored and freedom identified with social coercion. According to Burke the ideal of freedom and the inevitability of coercion are combined.

Is there no other way out? It looks like we are led to a spot where no objectivity concerning the meaning of freedom is possible. If we are to restore society to the theory of the Enlightenment, and fill the vacuum they left, must we give up the conception of freedom as an external matter and accept the definition of liberty as an internalized emancipation of the individual? This second view of freedom might seem the inevitable consequence of the restoration of society, yet we will try to retain the Enlightenment attitude toward freedom as emancipation from external force and still retain the significance of social facts.

Despite what the philosophes believed, society is inevitably coercive and therefore we must introduce it. Yet liberty can be viewed either as an absence of social restraint or as the internal presence of spiritual flowering. The problem only seems to be hopeless. Even the self-willed coercion of Rousseau is still coercive. The Enlightenment concept of liberty as the absence of restraint can be maintained, and therefore both Burke and Rousseau repudiated, while at the same time society can be reintroduced.

If the impact of society on the individual were monolithic there could be no escaping from the conclusions of Rousseau and Burke. But this is never the case. Even in nonliterate societies the influence of culture is always a plural one. While there cannot be an absence of social restraint, there are alternative forms of social controls as well as organizational impact. The Enlightenment concept of freedom can be saved; the individual masters society, sets himself against it, by dividing it against itself—not by eliminating it.

Let us take an economic example: a producer cannot escape the impact of organizational coercions. He must get a job and submit to authority. But an individual can move from factory A to factory B. In this way he can in a sense escape from the force of both factories; the reality of choice is decisive. While we must acknowledge the influence of the structure of the social order the ethical norm of the Enlightenment retains it validity.

Freedom for an individual lies in the cracks and crevices of a society; at every point at which a community is divided against itself the individual can be free. Liberty is neither escape from society nor identical with it. Freedom lies in the absence of social restraint made possible by alternative organizational coercions. The meaningful choice between alternative social forms, in this example the capacity to move from A to B, means there is a plural nature within the social order; this both provides an escape from an intellectual impasse and corresponds to our real experience of freedom.

We should not think of freedom as the absence of society; a sensation of liberty must be within a social order. Rousseau wrote that "the Englishman is only free at election times." Yet there are equivalents of elections in personal life. Consciousness of choice, for instance, conditions the behavior of both boss and employee, and the existence of alternatives is relevant in affecting the coercions of family life too. These moments of personal elections, taking place within social coercions and based on the presence of alternatives, are not exhausted in the making of the choices themselves; the possibility of choice exerts a continuous force on potential and actual facts.

Freedom is superlatively a matter of more or less, of movement between alternatives and the capacity for leverage. We must seek to create islands of freedom in a sea of coercion. Given the nature of society, liberty is always a question of degree. Any definition of freedom as an absolute is a barrier to understanding the need for its redefinition. Absolutist terms lead to Locke or Rousseau, the view that you have or do not have it as a whole. We must reject puristic notions of freedom. Liberty is a relative matter and based on the fluidity of the social order.

Patrick Henry's "Give me liberty or death!" is a pure fiction and a misleading slogan. In actual life it is never the situation one confronts; perfect freedom is impossible, and the presence of too many alternatives would lead to mental dizziness. Freedom has to be also a matter of small degree. The number of coercions over which an individual can have no elective power is large. The role of the family, from childhood to maturity, is beyond the capacity of choice. No one elects his early family constellation, and yet it is the greatest social power an individual confronts. We start life without the capacity of choice.

The Enlightenment's concept of freedom has to be so redefined that the ideal critical of the social environment is retained within the context of a real society. We are trying to synthesize the moral insights of the philosophes with the valid empirical perceptions of Rousseau. The philosophes missed the boat because the Enlightenment would have had to recognize the inevitability of society's coercions, and given up the ideal of unity; they would have had to recognize the plurality of organized centers of coercion. But they wanted to get away from multiplicity, since it threatened to bring them back to the old corporate society. We, however, must return to their hated pluralism and the institutional setup associated with the ideal of social alternatives.

Burke's whole attitude toward the social order was connected with his identifying liberty with internal freedom. While he was using these concepts traditionalistically we must adapt them. He insisted that we had to love "the little platoons" to which we belong. Society was for him made up of a series of links, such as class, church, or corporation; and he thought we should love each little link to which we are attached, since through such bonds the individual finds freedom. One might ask why love should not be directed at the general will of society, and why the experience of moral liberty should arise by virtue of an association with the peasantry, for example? He thought that the people, in order to fulfill themselves in this kind of freedom, need guidance; he proposes the idea of a natural aristocracy. Hierarchy was for him instrumental in individual liberation. Furthermore, since he thought that the sentiment of social solidarity can be overextended, he emphasized that it was easier to think in terms of a local group. Rousseau too had been troubled by the problem of solidarity; it was a sentiment, he thought, that could not be extended beyond a small state. He could not tolerate the decentralization of solidarity, and had to nationalize it; Rousseau's answer to the dilemma was nationalism. Burke, however, proposed to justify the small units within the old social order, and Burke was right. Solidarity is better maintained if bonds run among the family rather than to an abstraction like mankind.

One can grant Burke's point on the significance of the sentiment of solidarity and still question why the old feudal order has to be needed. The love of small associations is meaningful, but still the rigidities of all the components of corporate society is not a proper corollary. An individual may cease to love the blacksmith world because of the possibility of becoming a carpenter; this is both likely and desirable. For the old corporate order collapsed precisely because of an excess of crystallization of passions around the local corporations of society; it was this problem of becoming static that elicited the radical drive for unity. Class feelings, group hatreds, and the concomitant passions can so disintegrate a social system that an anti-group yearning for unity is almost inevitable. In France love of the whole was lacking because of excessive emotional attachments to the parts.

In our redefining freedom a certain amount of social movement between groups seems to breed the love of everyone; open alternatives lead away from overconcentrations in separate units. A flexible, pluralistic society strengthens social cohesion. X hates Y as long as there is a great gulf between them so that they look like another portion of society. We must respect the Burkean desire to maintain independent groups, and yet repudiate the fixity of separate elements in the corporate system. Totalitarian communities in our time, such as Fascism, can be caused by too much pluralism as well as too little of it. Class war means that there is an unfree plurality. The American experience indicates that as long as the laborer can become a capitalist, class war is minimized. It is slavelike coercive plurality that produces totalitarianism.

Rousseau was reacting against the unfree plurality of the old corporate system, and therefore he rejected the Enlightenment. He developed a concept of a unified society; his hatred of pluralism produced his notion of the General Will. What he really abhorred was unfree plurality, for free multiplicity would make everyman the potential brother of everyone. The possibility of movement makes for coworkers and allies. Rousseau was on a misguided search; the choice was not pluralism as opposed to unity, but free pluralism combined with unity in contrast to unfree pluralism and disintegration. Pluralism remains poorly understood, so that too little attention gets paid to the differences between fixed corporate pluralism and fluid liberal plurality.

Historically, in England, Burke's problem was that of rigidifying the Enlightenment, not just repudiating its antagonism to the old corporate order. But Locke's contracturalism was embarrassing; the right of withdrawal, combined with the fiduciary relationship between the state and society, meant that the public could take away its trust and overthrow the government. Burke set out to extract Locke's contract theory from its dangers and "solved" the problem by means of rhetoric. Burke claimed to believe in contract theory, but defined it as a partnership between generations, extending from the living to the dead to those not yet born. Only in a romantic, metaphorical sense did Burke mean a contract. This is not at all what Locke had had in mind; he had been trying to dissolve the influence of the past. Jefferson was a true Lockian when he wrote that "the earth belongs to the living." Burke was out of the world of Locke and the Enlightenment, and instead breathed the conservative spirit of Hooker and Disraeli. It had been purely a rhetorical device on Burke's part to propose a partnership of a historical type in order to undermine Locke.

Burke's special respect for the past, a perversion of Locke, deserves our reflection. A major strand in the history of political thought seeks to recapture the past; Renaissance writers such as Machiavelli, as well as Montesquieu, and also Rousseau with his classicism, appear to share this view of things. Burke seems to do so also; he differentiated the Revolution of 1688 and that of 1789 on the grounds that 1688 went back to English traditions, while 1789 was a violation of French history. But the concept of going back to search for legitimacy was difficult for Burke as a conservative; it is potentially revolutionary, and Tom Paine pointed out that if you go back far enough you can destroy the whole status quo. The Jacobins were great classicists; they were so reactionary that they succeeded in exploding French society. Going backwards becomes impossible ultimately for the conservative. Herbert Agar and his agrarian allies are real reformers; in wanting to get back to Jefferson they would succeed in destroying our society. The notion of returning to ancient virtues is technically not good for the conservative. The true conservative must have a concept of development to justify the present as well as the past; he must be able to say that the movement from Jefferson to Franklin D. Roosevelt, for example, is a good one. Burke did in fact believe in the providential development of society, and that progress was a result of history; he held that by means of traditional customs the social order was guided by Providence.

Burke's concept of prescription was remarkable; he held that institutions get their legitimacy from their ancient lineage. But prescription would seem to justify almost anything, making any old practice acceptable. Even the will to have majority rule would be justified if it were traditional. It appears he meant to use the notions of reason and habit interchangeably. In writing about the function of prescription Burke was emphasizing a factor having a great deal of empirical truth; Hume had also talked about the role of habit and tradition. Yet Burke did not inquire into the breakdown of prescription. He does not say why habits break down, which should have been his central preoccupation, but confines himself to how prescription functions.

Prejudices and prescriptions collapse when they become so out of tune with basic desires that the gap is intolerable; but traditions survive as long as they correspond to fundamental needs. There can be remarkable cultural lags, which Veblen understood. But the gulf between habit and desire can become unbearable. When the contrast between tradition and satisfaction is too great, rational inquiry begins; and metaphysicians attack the social habit and revolt against custom. But Burke could not see this.

Burke illustrates the general failure of the Reaction to grasp the elements of thought and aspiration as social facts. The Enlightenment and the Reaction produced two perspectives with dual limitations that are curiously balanced. Burke attacks the philosophes in behalf of the significance of social coercion, sentiment, and past traditions. He understands the organic aspects of community, the role of sentiment and feeling as a basic aspect of the social order, and the power of the traditions of the past. Burke pours back into the social emptiness of the philosophes those elements that Voltaire and the Enlightenment had eliminated. What they emptied he fills for us. Burke differs from Rousseau in that the Frenchman was still a part of the eighteenth-century Enlightenment and therefore stopped halfway with his concept of a solidaristic society. He had democratized and nationalized what the Enlightenment had left out. Burke always attacked Rousseau, though they both were performing the same operation of filling the sociological void left by the Enlightenment. Rousseau was unjustly dealt with on all sides. Burke was determined to fully restore the old society of classes and order and a corporatist state; he was willing to defend a ramshackle set of traditions.

So far we have encountered three possibilities; the Enlightenment's lack of social realism, Rousseau's solidaristic conception, and Burke's defense of traditional society. These three alternatives do not exhaust the intellectual options; and we shall be trying to see whether it proves possible to erect a fourth image that is different from the others and yet succeeds in carrying forward the ethical principles of the Enlightenment.

10

Joseph de Maistre

The Reaction attacked the Enlightenment at its weakest point and succeeded in bringing into question its ideals. Rousseau, however, played a key role in the story, by virtue of his social insight, linking eighteenth-century thought with the Reaction.

Maistre was a great political philosopher who articulated a passionate affirmation of royal sovereignty that cannot be found in the British strain of conservatism. The association of conservatism with absolute royal power is a distinctive French contribution. Such a theory of sovereignty would seem antithetical to the spirit of the old corporate world. The philosophes had seen the state as the instrument for the destruction of the quasi-feudal system. After the Revolution the old orders—the monarchy, the nobility, and the Church—made an alliance in behalf of the supposed restoration of absolutism. The Reaction supported monarchical power in a common attack against the new tide of democracy; the ideal of unitary sovereignty was advanced to protect the old order, as a technique of the Enlightenment was now used against it. The ancien régime now saw that its real enemy was democracy. The Revolution had substituted a new struggle for the old one. In the creation of this fresh conflict the monarchy realized that it was enmeshed in the system it had sought to destroy, and that the ancien régime had a common enemy in democracy.

The only shelter for tradition seemed to lie in absolute monarchy. The clue to the eventual defeat of the Reaction, the

new alliance that came alive under the aegis of restored Bour-
bonism, was that absolute monarchy proved not strong enough.
By now the middle class could stand on its own feet, and it was
looking in a different direction.

Even though it is often alleged that the establishment of the
concept of absolute sovereignty is easy, when the liberals had
used it in the eighteenth century they encountered difficulties.
The physiocrats had judges set up over their supposedly absolute sovereign. As a moral basis for the claim to absolute
sovereignty, Maistre rested his case on the familiar bifurcation
of personality, also found in Burke, of a higher and a lower self.
Conscience was opposed to interest, and reason at odds with
passion. Mastery by the higher self, made up of the controls
over prejudice and emotion, was to come about through sovereignty. Maistre casts the familiar psychological dualism in a
theological mold. Inner mastery of the individual is not possible
by the individual himself. In Maistre the sovereign is the instrument for moral liberation; the sovereign makes certain that the
higher self is triumphant over impulses in revolt. Rousseau's
dualistic conception was here being implemented by absolutism. His rational will became transformed into external force
in Maistre; with Rousseau the idea had been the self-imposition
of moral will, self-mastery, but that humanitarian-sounding
ethic was replaced by Maistre's authoritarianism.

Maistre's logic seems iron-clad and was theological in origin.
He insisted on the corruption of man, the original Fall of human
beings, and the consequent inner evil. Men were divided into
higher and baser beings by traditional Christian thinking; Rousseau's thought was secular in separating the rational and particular will. Maistre made the familiar distinction of different
selves in connection with the theological system that begins
with Original Sin. The individual was for Maistre saddled with
intrinsic evil; the cure lay in God functioning through the
secular sovereign. In this way the individual could be compelled to emancipate himself from individual sin.

Two consequences followed. First of all, self-government of
any kind is impossible since Maistre's view eliminates the internal character of any drive toward good. The cure for evil cannot
come from within; the remedy must be external to man. Sec-

ondly, the sovereign as God's agent must be not only apart from man but unlimited; any restrictions on his power would impair its externality. The subject can only be saved through outside action. Man's incapacity would interfere if he could influence the sovereign; internal evil requires the external agent of absolutism. To compromise sovereignty would be to limit this externality, and therefore weaken what is needed to check evil.

What assurances exist that the sovereign will justify his moral basis? Maistre's theological purpose in using divine law was a shadow of the physiocratic dilemma of relying on natural law. It had been tempting to redefine absolutism by empowering magistrates in order to be sure that the sovereign will really pursue his end; the tension between power and legitimacy was not resolved in the eighteenth century. Maistre's radical solution was to argue that the sovereign, being single, will be disinterested when confronted by a multiplicity of cases, hence more likely to fulfill divine will. The more people involved the more prone authority is to corruption; he was suspicious of the many interests in society. He consequently attacked Rousseau for his concept of democracy. The Reaction abhorred Rousseau, yet they obviously incorporated his ideas into their conservative theories. Rousseau had proposed a democratic society; the Reaction hated the democratic part but liked the emphasis on the social component and absolute sovereignty.

Maistre further argued that even if the sovereign acts unjustly, he still would be exercising the divine purpose. He took the implacable position that all injustice is itself something to be desired as the vengeance of God on man for his degradation, the payment for his bondage to interest rather than conscience. Power is therefore justified by means of asserting that the purposes of God are complex.

Maistre was fascinated with violence and brutality in and of itself. He seemed romantically to surrender to brutality, and had an almost Darwinian sense of the struggle between all species in life. Later, D. G. Ritchie, a Darwinian, got into trouble trying to prove that the fittest would survive by means of a process of competitive destruction. The question also arises in Maistre of whether what is done will be the right thing; Maistre's ruthless logic conceded that even the best will die in this universal slaughter. But the decimation of the finest was a working out of a divine scheme, the penalty God imposed for man's Fall. Maistre gave himself up to accident; the anguish of the innocent atoned for the sins of the guilty. The just pay the price for the unjust.

Maistre's was a tightly constructed theory. Even if the sovereign is apparently unrighteous he serves a moral purpose in functioning as an instrument of an inscrutable deity. Yet Maistre's thought is not so hard to undermine; for, just at this point when the door is shutting, the house begins to collapse. What happens to Maistre's claims for the justification of the legitimacy of the sovereign? The Revolution had after all supplanted a pious king with an impious revolutionary leader. The suffering of a Bourbon monarch could after all be the workings of a mysterious God, and the revolutionaries could be the avengers of God. Maistre's outlook meant an abandonment to complete irrationality in connection with the exercise of power. By accepting injustice and the way God works inscrutably through violence, Maistre undermined the basis for his own claims in behalf of legitimacy. It became impossible for him to sustain a distinction between what he liked and what he hated. A fine example of the reversability of Maistre's principle could be the French Revolution itself: God working through violence.

Maistre was so anxious to close the gap between power and legitimacy that he undermined legitimacy itself. Hobbes, too, failed to distinguish between power and right; he also had wanted sovereignty to eliminate struggle. Yet it is always proper to ask what moral claims an existing authority has to power. Ethics and power are logically in tension; if one is identified with the other, then it raises the question of whether those you support have a legitimate right to govern. The purpose of political philosophizing—the distinction between something right and something wrong—is then gone.

Every absolutist theorist has something of this same relation to the concept of sovereignty; maybe a particular sovereign will do damage to what the thinker wants to promote. It was certainly a fear of the physiocrats. Maistre was of course not a liberal economist but a Catholic; but an absolute sovereign may not in all cases serve the Catholic purpose.

Maistre's position also involved the supreme claim of Papal rule known as Ultramontane supremacy. He repudiated traditional Gallic liberties, wanting to revert to the high medieval period and cede power to the Pope to control and depose monarchs, as in Innocent III's old claims. Maistre made the Pope absolute, the apex of unity. But the logic of absolute power cannot survive this theory; the Papacy merely replaces the dilemma of the physiocratic judges. Papal power broke down when the absolute monarch became as powerful as Maistre wanted it. Authority was checked by authority because of fear of what absolute sovereignty might do. It is impossible to avoid the gap between power and legitimacy, and it is therefore difficult for an absolutist to stick to unity. The Papacy could not establish such power in the nineteenth century. Maistre was working with a conflicting set of principles, two absolute monarchs. Absolutism is a hard principle to establish; it may sound like a simple idea, but it does not have any simplicity in terms of its implementation.

Maistre was using theology more deftly when he proposed a religious basis for the unity of the state; he found it in Catholicism. The reactionary trend of thought was moving in on the social void of the Enlightenment. He stressed, in contrast to Voltaire, the necessary element of mythology in society; Voltaire may have been party to an irresponsible rationalism but Maistre went on to defend the Inquisition. He borrowed Rousseau's argument for civil religion to support the logic of theological intolerance against evil. He wanted to see the higher will triumph, and in its behalf the morality of the Inquisition was restored.

How do we avoid these three images of society? Given the necessity of religion and myth, the idea of intellectual liberty appears to be an impossibility. But it is not necessary to choose between Maistre's brand of religion and the unreal situation in Voltaire's thought. Every society must have suprarational symbols. Man's freedom of mind lies, however, not in escape but in the power to exchange one set of symbols for another. The struggle comes in splitting myths into pieces to create alternatives that give meaning to freedom. We can retain the negative concept of freedom by stressing the power of society to alter the symbols by which it lives. Becker wrote about how the eighteenth century had deified nature while stripping God from its thinking. The human mind is inherently limited by mythical systems; however, imaginative intellectual experience creates new myths for old ones.

A free society must have in its myth one fixed point that cannot be changed: the freedom to question the myth. This has to be a permanent part of the liberal mythological world. If men want to change this fixed point, liberalism has a basic problem. It is an open question whether we should, for example, extend freedom of speech to Communists and Fascists. The principle of alternatives has to end somewhere; or is it itself perhaps only one of our alternatives? We can provide no solution to this fundamental dilemma.

Maistre had, besides the problem of myth, raised the issue of history and tradition. He shared Burke's attachment to the past, which was an admission that the old theological basis for politics was no longer sufficient. Conservatives have a special problem in that they cannot use the past as a norm without difficulty, because it involves a retrogressive revolution that threatens to destroy the status quo. The past is as revolutionary as the future. A concept of development is forced on conservatives in order for history to be used to justify the present. Burke wrote about the past of nations being guided by Providence.

Maistre emphasized the generative principle of constitutional form. Men can succeed in changing minor things politically, conventional laws, but major constitutional matters develop according to Providence. There is no possibility of emancipating us from history. This idea was like the Burkean notion of prescription; the present was thereby being legitimized. Maistre held that the concept that men can create constitutions in violation of history is untenable. It would contradict the determinism of Providential purpose. He was stressing a significant point, particularly plausible as a response to the experience of the eighteenth century; no one can create constitutions out of whole cloth. This was part of the objection John Adams raised against Paine; the strength of the American constitution was in fact its continuity with old colonial usages.

Still, Maistre's insight does not rule out the historic existence of revolutions; the Reaction was right, the French Revolution had failed, but it still wrought great changes, though not as many as the revolutionaries had expected. The desire to create a new political system did succeed in radically affecting Puritan England, and Russia in 1917. Revolutionary upheaval would be unlikely if people did not in fact cherish the dream of impossible social transformations; the tremendous changes in France after 1789 took place because the revolutionaries nourished the fallacy that they could alter even more. Aspiration had to exceed their reach. The historical fact of such desire widens the scope of possibility. The arguments of Burke and Maistre about the inconceivability of changing societal forms is therefore seriously challenged and does not successfully rule out revolution as a legitimate weapon. They misunderstood the quality of aspiration and the indeterminancy of action; the Reaction could not genuinely understand revolution.

If history is the expression of divine Providence, then that has also to embrace the Enlightenment and its Revolution as part of God's will. Maistre cannot recognize this because he aims to establish an older order. But his attitude toward the eighteenth century was as blind as the eighteenth century's own attitude toward its past. For the Providential movement does not stop; if what takes place is that which is Providentially determined, the criterion is: whatever happens. By Maistre's own logic the Revolution becomes justified as part of Providential development and the past, which is never static, swallows up the present. In surrendering to inscrutable Providential determinism in order to escape the past he disapproved of, Maistre was also giving up what he would most like to defend. The Reaction could not really use history or development out of the past, for history is always ethically neutral. It is difficult if not impossible for anyone to cling to the present. The whole search for fixity contradicts the world of change in which we live. The moment reactionaries want to hold on to will never survive; the present instance cannot be frozen.

Like his Enlightenment predecessors Maistre inquired into nature and its law. He thought that the law of nature was to be discovered in the anatomy of man; it would then be reflected in empirical behavior. The state of nature is artificial. But despite what Maistre thought this was no way of undermining Rousseau—for he did not seek to go back to nature as an objective, and he did not wish to retain the freedom of nature for society. Locke, Turgot, and the Enlightenment invoked the virtues of the state of nature; Maistre was really responding to them when he maintained that man can have no natural rights in society, for the social order is natural to him.

Maistre was holding that man was made for social relations; the law of nature was revealed in the impact of society on man. Bonald too believed that the law of nature was a good concept and revealed empirically. History becomes in Maistre a technique for discovering the laws of nature. This idea that the past should be studied as the handmaiden of political science is really the beginning of the world of Comte and modern social science.

The philosophes had used the concept of nature both normatively and empirically to reason away society; although they started with a Newtonian view of nature as empirical, they shifted to invoking it normatively. During the Reaction, however, the emphasis was all on fact. The conservatives spoke of existence as if it were inherently normative, and thus they eliminated the independence of values. The Reaction did not attack the basic methodology of the Enlightenment but advanced it by inverting the concept of nature like an hourglass and reasoning away the distinction between facts and norms. Empirical reality was supposedly ethically compelling.

The secret of the Reaction lies in the Enlightenment it was responding to. The failure of conservatives to understand the aspirations of man was associated with the peculiar concept of nature it got from the eighteenth century. Burke understood habit but not why people ever revolt against custom. And Maistre did not understand why history changes. We are still left with a triangular situation—liberty without society, a solidaristic kind of totalitarianism, or a traditionalistic sociology.

It should nonetheless be possible to retain the ideals of the philosophes without giving in to the solution of the Enlightenment, Rousseau, or the Reaction. One first has to break out of the whole natural law way of thinking, which made it possible to evade the real problem that must be confronted. Both ideals and reality have to be retained, and the qualities of aspiration as well as submission understood, in order to achieve a democratic sociology. Change and stability play their parts in history. The natural law method has to be abandoned if we are to appreciate that the problem of facts and values is not solved by the identification of the one with the other. A perpetual tension exists between norm and fact, even though both the philosophes and the conservatives sought to eliminate the issue in the pursuit of Nirvana.

11

Louis de Bonald

Like other conservatives Bonald assailed the Enlightenment at its strategic weakness; in many ways we find a duplication of Maistre, although Bonald is more systematic. He put society back but also proved that it could not be altered. He was fascinated with the number three, and talked about the triad of cause, means, and effect. Because society is divine, the means (His agent) becomes absolute, and the effect is man himself. Human beings are the product of the sovereign acting under the cause of society, which is God. Society creates man, and man cannot alter it. Bonald reduced human beings to subservient instruments of society. Bonald had other triads as well—father, mother, and children, and God, priests, and believers. Most importantly for our purposes, Bonald considered man impotent before the cause and the means.

Therefore the whole of society comes back. The individual cannot have any rights against the social order. Society becomes an organic entity with a will and life of its own, independent of the individuals composing it; this is a distinctive element that cannot be found in Maistre or Burke. Also like neither Maistre or Burke, Bonald is a clear disciple of Rousseau. The same concepts are there in Bonald as in Rousseau; the binding force of society, which Rousseau called the General Will, instead in Bonald is the monarchy. Rousseau's popular sovereignty yields to Bonald's monarch; the structure of a General Will supports them both. Bonald, like Rousseau, proposed a conflict between the General Will and the particular will of men; particularity is demonstrated when the will of the sovereign is opposed, and rationality is present when the sovereign is obeyed. Man is involved in an inner struggle between his individualism, which constitutes his desire to destroy, and his natural social constitution.

It is reasonable to wonder why, since human beings are created by the sovereign who in turn is God's instrument, man should ever be compelled to revolt. According to Bonald the explanation lies in the original Fall, man's basic depravity. Just as man, who is created by God, revolts against Him, so human beings, made by society, rebel against the social order. Rousseau had secularized this notion from Christian dogma. In Bonald, when it comes to man's revolt against the social system, there is almost no analysis; sin is taken as an explanatory fact. Yet the way in which society shapes man in its image is documented in good sociological fashion. Still, sinfulness is as much a fact as the force of society.

If creation by God can be studied sociologically surely sin can be as fruitful a starting point. But the reactionaries did not wish to study sin. It would have led them, had they examined it with the same sociological passion, to have found a counterpart in revolution for creation. The conservatives wanted to avoid this since it exposed the peculiar deficiency of the Reaction in its understanding of society. The aspirational aspect of man—that which can judge, change, perhaps destroy society—is an aspect of reality missing in Bonald. Yet he was the most thoroughgoing social scientist of the Reaction.

His whole approach to history was static. If a thinker does not have a theory of change and is a reactionary, he confronts certain special dilemmas. As events move from A to B and then on to C, one might want to defend B. Bonald rejected the concept of going from A to B, and the notion of development; he had a stationary outlook, and was not concerned with Providential flow. He was able to stick to the status quo with more rigor since he had not created a developmental monster. Bonald held that tradition as it has stopped at any point must be preserved; according to him it embraces everything and comprehends the complexity of society.

Language was a key for Bonald. It was to him the root of man's thought since we think words before ideas. Man also could not have created language, since he would need the thought of creation first. Language was in Bonald's view a divine gift, the essence of tradition since man cannot control it. Bonald's approach was dubious and has seriously been challenged by students of linguistics; yet it comprised a critical argument by which he arrived at the conclusion that man is enslaved to tradition and society.

Bonald's theory about language fitted into his conviction about the absolute domination of tradition; in contrast, Condorcet thought the meaning of tradition lay in its dissolution. As Burke on the matter of organization and Maistre with the issue of myth, Bonald concentrated on the notion of tradition. He poured back the social reality that the Enlightenment had eliminated. Burke reintroduced corporate classes and organizational coercion; Maistre brought back religion and mythical constraints; Bonald, in a battle against Condorcet, established the complete tyranny of tradition.

With Bonald we face the same resolution to the problem posed in the context of the other conservative thinkers; there is a solution for us midway between the position of Bonald and that of Condorcet. The framework of alternatives is the one in which we must work. Man is never wholly emancipated from tradition, yet freedom lies in his capacity to alter it when the drive to do so asserts itself. When men are really free they can substitute one set of traditional practices for another, not that they can escape all tradition. For the new tradition that men have created shortly becomes as tyrannical as an old tradition. The problem should repeat itself of the exchange of traditions.

In the early nineteenth century the concept of "free contract" had a certain reality; yet soon the idea became a justification for economic tyranny. Veblen's theory of cultural lag is precisely what is relevant to the experience of the exchange of cultural traditions. Liberty implies no goal but rather a process, an unending activity, not "free contract," but rather freedom to have or reject the doctrine of "free contract." New traditions will be as burdensome as old ones. We are talking about the perpetual repetition, the renewal of old struggles; in the exercise of choice lies the heart of liberty.

In contrast, the Enlightenment saw freedom as an absolute

goal to be gotten and then held. The philosophes shared an essential lack of realism. They wanted to smash the old order to attain liberty. Their approach was wrong, because the meaning of freedom lies in a process. If liberty is defined as meaningful choice, the selection of alternatives, we can reintroduce all the necessary social materials. For Condorcet history came to an end in a final epoch; a different concept of freedom entails the permanence of pain and tension.

As similar in many ways as Bonald was to the other theorists of the Reaction, he had a different orientation to method. Burke was the orator of conservatism, Maistre the poet, and Bonald the social scientist. He wrote in a turgid and dull manner, proceeding with a steamroller quality. Given the structure of reactionary thought it might seem questionable whether there was any room for social science. The Reaction emphasized the intuitive elements of social behavior, and therefore would seem to repudiate social science. It stressed the inscrutable, indefinable qualities in social life, and expressed an unscientific orientation. Maistre insisted that men cannot create constitutions by any rational act but must simply accept them. Burke proposed that leadership involved an intuitive element, and that therefore we need aristocracy rather than brain-trusters.

Even though human beings cannot change society, the Reaction assumes that it is possible for man to accumulate much knowledge about why he cannot alter it. This impossibility of changing the social order can be documented in a scientific way. The impact of society on man to the extent that it determines his behavior yields a wealth of empirical analysis; the Reaction thus did offer a great impetus to the development of social science.

The Enlightenment had its influence on the Reaction methodologically. Bonald searched for universal laws, and he repudiated Montesquieu for his relativism. Bonald was involved in a search for universality, but he was looking for empirical laws that had been eliminated by the "science" of the Enlightenment. He attempted to discover empirical uniformities in actual social systems to undermine the universal laws advanced by the Enlightenment. The philosophes were not alone in their pretenses to science. Both sides search for universals; the Reaction looked for broad principles exposing the enslavement of man to society.

The conservatives inverted the natural law technique to defend the social system; facts became a norm. In both the Enlightenment and the Reaction the search for universal laws proceeds. With Comte the indebtedness will be to both Condorcet and Bonald; Comte was a founder of social science, and not superficially reactionary. In social thought today much liberal political thinking still fears that social knowledge will threaten its idealism. And students of social facts likewise have the feeling that their discovery somehow is an ethical end.

The main theoretical techniques of the revolutionary theorists were adopted by the reactionaries, and have continued to be models both on the Left and the Right. The Enlightenment had used nature normatively and empirically, confusing a central distinction; the Reaction did not repudiate this, but exploited it in an inverted way. The reactionaries seized on facts and elevated them as norms. In order to escape from both utopianism and blind conservatism we need to give up the whole natural law confusion of the "ought" and the "is." The Reaction was blind because it eliminated the drive for the ideal, just as the Enlightenment had excluded the empirical and practical problems of myths, economic coercion, and history.

12

Auguste Comte

In Germany the Reaction, at least in Hegel, will become relatively progressive. But it was in France that conservatism was really reactionary, and Bonald and Maistre constituted the heart of it.

Although Auguste Comte was an authoritarian, he worked under the influence of some eighteenth-century theorists. In connection with individualism he was an opponent of the Enlightenment's libertarianism. But he did not cast his thought in a theological mold; rather he expressed it as a scientific counterpart to Bonald's notions of sin and creation. Armed with the rationalistic spirit of the philosophes Comte proposed to study the impact of social factors on individuals. With him the theology of the other conservatives was gone, and we are left with an exclusive concentration on the scientific study of the influence of society. He eliminated the theological framework and adopted the task of empirical investigations.

He pursued the concept of an observable natural law in society. Man has a personal and a social impulse; the former drive is the stronger by nature, and therefore in order to survive people must cooperate and thus expand the social propensity. The survival of the individual and the exploitation of nature lead to the progressive expansion of the social impulse over the personal one. Wherever the social order exists, fostering the communal impulse, the principle of command and obedience will inevitably be present. The archetype for such inequality can be found in feudal organization—authoritarian religious and political power.

Comte undermined atomic individualism and restored the old society with its hierarchies. He pursued the normal reactionary path in turning back to the old society of a medieval type. Yet he assailed the hopes of the traditionalists who wanted to go back to the old order either theologically or secularly. Maistre could have little popular appeal in the nineteenth century. Comte repudiated the Reaction on the grounds that it is impossible to stop history, and he was perfectly correct.

The rise of industrialism and the coming of its social problems established in some sense the validity of reactionary theory. For these thinkers had supported the significance of the stuff and structure of society; industrialism was a social system ignored by the Enlightenment. Yet at the same time these new developments were damaging to conservatives, for the industrial revolution ultimately could not be contained within the moral framework of the ancien régime.

Comte advanced a new order to serve the purpose of social cohesion, but he proposed to incorporate fresh economic material. He thought government should be concentrated in the hands of a new capitalist class to fight both the proletariat and the bourgeoisie who were expressing merely a personal drive. This rule in behalf of social order would take place paternally, pleasantly, and to Comte it represented the social impulse. The proletariat's fight against capitalism must be stopped; this personal drive was to be submerged in the acceptance of paternal guidance. Comte had in mind reintroducing the old spiritual power exercised by the priests in order to preach the highly authoritarian principle of humanity embodied in his positive science. He cherished the authoritarian structure of society as an ideal image, yet sought to use the new industrial materials of the nineteenth century in adapting the old conception.

In advocating a corporate organization of industrial life Comte had in mind a good totalitarian state; his proposal bore a resemblance to modern Fascism. Comte's system also prefigured some of English conservatism, for Carlyle and Disraeli advanced an outlook of feudal industrialism: capitalism was to be contained within a quasi-medieval structure having British industrialists as a new aristocratic order. This theoretical tack meant absorbing the nineteenth-century world into the old reactionary system. But such corporate industrialism did not work; the proletariat would not accept it, for they had already been indoctrinated with the egalitarian ideals of the eighteenth century.

The conservatives could not undo the work of the Revolution with respect to the proletariat. The ideals of liberty, equality, and fraternity were now a permanent goal in modern thought. Marx possessed this critical insight; in *Das Kapital* he demonstrated that he understood how the proletariat was irrevocably wedded to egalitarian liberalism. Marxism came to terms with the revolutionary dilemma: the proletariat would accept no theory that did not incorporate the normative principles of the Revolution, yet by its existence as a class it refuted the egalitarian doctrine that tried to evade their coming into being. The problem was that of implementing the ideals of the Enlightenment in the context of the real world. The ethical heritage of the eighteenth century could not be undone, yet the compulsion to solve the social problem was also permanent. It was necessary to face the issue of coercion in terms of eighteenth-century ideals.

Comtian method proposed a philosophy of positivism as social science. Since he stressed the significance of sociology in human affairs and the presence of social constraints, he was moving in the direction of modern social science. He hypothesized three stages of history: theological, metaphysical, and positivistic. The theological was the most primitive since it involved religion as a technique to link men together; according to Comte, theology was a component of the social instinct generated by the need for survival. In the movement from polytheism to monotheism, the "critical spirit" appeared, making possible the perception of a wider range of uniformity. The critical spirit was abstract and generalizing; it widened the bonds holding men together, producing a larger community. In making these ties wider it weakened them; we have here a repetition of a familiar theme that arose in Rousseau and Burke: the broader the bond the more fragile the community. For Comte the growth of the critical spirit thus undermines society.

The critical spirit ushered in the metaphysical era and the concept of natural law; for Comte this stage is most destructive of society. The critical spirit has potentialities for construction yet not in this phase. It still retains the character of theology; its laws are not those of actual behavior; they advance nonempirical propositions that are perpetual invitations to social disobedience. First, the right of private judgment as a mandate of natural law, which occurs in Voltaire, unsettles the whole fabric of society and the possibility of agreement on principle. Secondly, the idea that all men are born equal overlooks the presence of inequality in society. And thirdly, the belief in popular sovereignty proves impossible since command and obedience must always be necessary. Laws of nature, which represent the critical spirit in the metaphysical stage, are destructive; they function normatively, exploding the perpetual basis of any social system. By extending the critical spirit to the positive (by which he meant "actual") stage, Comte proposed to ally it with the realities of an ongoing social system. His analysis of the natural law school of thought was powerful; Becker echoed it when he wrote about the philosophes having substituted Nature for God.

Comte says that the ideals of the eighteenth century were associated with an absence of an understanding of any functioning society. In the metaphysical stage the critical spirit takes no account of any real social order. Comte's thinking is reminiscent of the whole drift of the Reaction, and especially of Bonald and Maistre. He accepted the eighteenth century's quest for universal laws and tried to make them empirical. He wanted to translate natural law onto a social plane. He was doing on a methodological level what the Reaction had done on a more abstract level.

There was an inner connection between the representative examples of the first stage and the Messiah of stage number three; for under positivism, generalizing intelligence finally gets used to discover the principles of real life. Theological atomism could be associated with and anticipate Comte himself because the Enlightenment had forced its categories on the Reaction. The conservatives had to speak in more than theological terms. After the philosophes one needed to have science as well as God, or some kind of rationalism combined with natural law. Comte and the conservatives bore the heritage of the Enlightenment; they sought to discover natural law of an empirical type. Bonald spoke in terms of creation and society, God as well as sociology; he was not merely a representative of the theological stage but a confirmation of it and the incipient positivist phase. When it came to Comte's stages, the first ultimately combined with the third, yet Comte never took this into account.

The Reaction did not destroy the confusion of fact and norm but merely inverted it. Comte denied falling into this fallacy too; he thought he had eliminated animism, done away with metaphysics, and introduced the significance of positive social fact. He wanted to get away from the norm-fact dualism, and instead stress the existence of the reality of society itself.

Yet Comte did precisely what the Reaction had done on its sociological side, and he did it patently. For all his social data he advanced a conservative norm. The individual, with the libertarian implications associated with the ideal, goes out. He thought that the discovery of social law would make people realize that they cannot accomplish much and thus kill the revolutionary impulse. A scientist only recognizes existence; but Comte read norms into his whole system. Positivism served as a normative social measure. He therefore fell into the same morass as the conservative movement; he elevated to the role of norm those facts eliminated by the eighteenth century.

The whole school of French positivism endorsed a principle of solidarity. They sold themselves out to a solidaristic norm they thought they had discovered. Their methodological impulse was to uncover the facts to refute the Enlightenment and omit considerations of the ideals of the Revolution as a fact. Instead they accepted some few facts as a norm; this inversion of eighteenth-century thought by the Reaction was carried forward in Comtian sociology without any serious alteration.

We have watched a giant teeter-totter based on natural law rock between the Enlightenment and the Reaction. The fact-value problem is to be resolved by the recognition that however related, they remain logically separate. The perpetual connection and separation cannot be obliterated; their simultaneous relatedness and disconnectedness has to be acknowledged.

Our norms are not self-effectuating. The values of individual liberty and equality, for example, are not immanent in reality; ideals must always be implemented. The Enlightenment's utopianism gave perpetual ammunition for the Reaction. But at the same time facts must always be evaluated. The presence of the social reality of cohesion, and the shaping force of society with which norms must struggle, does not settle any moral question. We should not jump into this realm and attach any value significance to facts, for while they are related, value and fact are forever disconnected.

Both implementation and evaluation are the whole essence of human life. The two operations are characteristic of living. These thinkers sought to eliminate the dilemmas of existence that come from perpetual tension. They were in search of Nirvana where the painful aspects of life will not be present; by eliminating processes of implementation and evaluation human beings could go to sleep. An underlying premise of the age was expressed in writers frantically seeking to feel free from the central responsibilities of existence.

We must break away from the methodological confusion of the era and its flight from reality. It is difficult to detach ourselves since it remains their historic bequest; modern categories of thought are derived from this heritage of the argument between the Enlightenment and the Reaction. Liberal thinkers are still apt to be embarrassed by social facts, and empirical students too often make a value out of their materials; these historic tendencies are directly relevant to politics and sociology as fields of study today. These different realms of discourse should be related so that neither will threaten the other but instead be mutually fortifying. There is no reason why the mood of political theory should be that of the Enlightenment. Constructive normative preoccupations should not be threatened by the necessity of social compulsion.

The treason of the intellectual can lie in his/her lack of responsibility. The adoption of either a utopian orientation or a reactionary perspective represents flight and escape. In the division of labor in society the intellectual is essentially involved in an ivory tower operation. Yet intellectuals must confront the problems that they deal with and repudiate both utopianism and a naive form of conservatism. What they do with this detachment is the clue to the possibility of their betraying their calling. Yet a steady confrontation of evaluation and implementation means a break with a tradition of modern political thought.

13

Georg W. F. Hegel

With Hegel in Germany we run into the problem again of the uniqueness of a writer, for the domestic setting of a nation will take a thinker, who is concerned with common philosophic problems, and twist him. In a country that lacked revolution, Hegel carried forward and transformed many ideas of the Reaction.

Hegel represents a different philosophy from that of the reactionaries we have discussed so far. He polemicized against the conservatives of the French type. He battled against the Swiss Karl Ludwig von Haller who advanced views like Bonald's: the traditional order is natural and hierarchy is inevitable and moral. Hegel assailed the old feudal order in the name of liberty, reason, and rights. He repudiated traditionalism. In his discussion of "civil society" in *The Philosophy of Right* he presented a picture of untrammelled individuals exercising particular wills in attaining their ends of private profits. His version of competitive individualism paralleled that of classical economics. He proposed a harmonious principle which was reminiscent of Smith and the physiocrats; Hegel thought that the competitive world is governed by an invisible hand of rationality. He was thereby challenging the conservatives, since they had denied the possibility of atomistic harmony and insisted upon the necessity of external coercion.

Hegel was outside the mood of the eighteenth century at the same time he was in it. According to him the mutual harmony ultimately breaks down and the outcome becomes accidental; arbitrary contingency develops, equity of treatment begins to disappear, coercions and misery arise, and the system transforms itself into an essentially capricious one on which the individual cannot rely for fulfillment. Hegel levels two indictments: mutual satisfaction becomes increasingly irrational, an affair of accident, not freedom, and capital breeds power and social inequality. Herbert Marcuse's interpretation of Hegel highlights the significance of his notion of the degeneration of society into the rich and the poor.

Actually Hegel anticipates Marx in an even wider setting. For sociology is, as we shall see, a prelude to Marxism. It is a myth that Hegel was unconcerned with a going society; an idealist can be realistic. Hegel thought that the world of social practice was the realization of ideal forms, but the institution of those forms can be ruthlessly pursued. Hegel was therefore acutely sensitive to the empirical developments of the nineteenth century.

He proceeded further than the eighteenth century; for as the "civil society" breaks down a new organizing scheme is needed, and he has in mind a system of estates. Hegel was concerned for everyone in the community in an effort to rescue people from the unregulated functioning of competition. He proposed a separate corporation for peasants, merchants, industrialists, and the bureaucracy. Corporate groupings were needed to protect its members from arbitrary action. By means of providing education, security, and status the individual would be supported and secured against contingency; each person becomes externally accepted by his neighbors, thereby legitimizing individuality. Wealth and poverty are authenticated by being integrated into a body meaningful in social terms. Spiritual supports come from the status of belonging to a group, which saves each individual from the sense of isolation arising from competition.

Hegel's resolution is reminiscent of the corporate ideal of the prerevolutionary era. Although he repudiates the rationalism of the eighteenth century, he ends up with the corporate ideal within the context of rationalism itself. It is a curiously Hegelian odyssey, for he hated feudalism as much as Rousseau. As a pupil of the Enlightenment Hegel reacts against the old system and penetrates the atomism of the philosophes; in seeing irrationality he returns to corporatism. He perceived that individualism had the makings for a genuine new society, yet it would not be as harmonious as the atomic image pretends, and therefore he constructed a new kind of corporatism.

Marcuse compared Hegel's corporate ideal with the collectivist state of the twentieth century. The objectives of status, social peace, and the freezing of society do sound like Mussolini's fascism. Comte's hierarchical system had the same root perception as in Hegel. Comte, however, repudiated feudalism, and wanted to work within the new society, as he aimed to reconstruct the old hierarchical structure within the context of industrialism. In England Carlyle and Disraeli advocated what Marx would call "feudal socialism"; they attempted to incorporate the materials of nineteenth-century industrialism into the traditionalistic categories.

Hegel, Comte, and Carlyle are so different that they generally cannot be put together. But they were deeply related in an effort to solve in a corporate way the problem of industrialism. They wanted to resolve the conflicts of nineteenth-century capitalism using a static approach, and to freeze industrial energies in a framework of corporate order. Their respective national settings become critical for understanding these writers: the feudal socialism of Disraeli shows how British conservatism attempted to absorb industrialism; Comte demonstrates how in France there was a special concern with theology; for Hegel the German feudal system was not shaken, and therefore he proposed the idea of the state.

Feudal socialism was a dubious solution to industrial problems. The Enlightenment conception of freedom had irrevocably penetrated the masses; they would not accept a proposal grounded on hierarchical ideas. The corporate approach lacked adequate social soil; the groups suffering most from disorganization had become permanently attached to the philosophy of the Enlightenment. Marx knew it, and his socialism had a much greater appeal than these corporate static systems. Socialism had its attraction because it promised to solve the same problem that Hegel, Comte, and Carlyle saw, but within the context of the ideals of the philosophes.

But even theoretically any social status-bound system would

fail to eliminate conflict as these reactionary writers wished; providing a corporate ground to industrialism would institutionalize strife rather than limit it. Burke had emphasized society as a series of platoons, but it is doubtful that they served his larger end. The frozen character of these platoons would make it difficult to move from one sector to another, defining personality wholly in terms of one group and provoking an intransigent response in another. A frozen pluralism is one that can itself engender violence. In contrast, free plurality, involving a measure of movement between groups, will limit any involvement in intergroup conflict and can achieve a larger unity.

The conservative solutions to the search for unity might have produced greater conflicts than the unrestrained working out of the nineteenth-century system. The later industrial peace of Italy and Germany lay not in their corporate system but in one-party, totalitarian political regimes.

Hegel did envisage something above his corporate system, which is where his concept of the state came in. A theory of freedom of movement as an instrument for achieving solidarity would have been shocking to him. In the tradition of Rousseau and Burke, Hegel defines freedom in terms of the exercise of rational will as opposed to the particularity of mere interest; outside coercion functions as the means of liberty. Hegel did not base his system on the use of corporations as instruments of liberalism; in his view they were wedded to an irrevocable narrowness of interest. The way to foster rational will is by external power, which could not be expected to come from corporations based on economic advantage. Another body was needed to serve the purpose of the General Will and to be unconcerned with economic ends: the state. As a member of the state the individual finds the rational will functioning; the state therefore regulates civil society.

It might appear that we have got back to Rousseau; for in Hegel, corporations are resolved into unity. Yet Rousseau's General Will flowed from the autonomous will of individuals; he had an individualistic starting point. His concern with self-imposed morality was to be carried forward by Kant. The heavy influence of Rousseau made Kant stick to individualism; yet Kant was still a monarchist frightened of revolution. Kant thought that if the General Will was not sovereign then the existing rules must be accepted; law became the source of right.

In transferring Rousseau from Paris to Germany there is an alteration that becomes major with Hegel: the individual stops being the point of departure of analysis; concern with the state became so great that he began with it and worked down to the individual. Civil society, an individualistic starting point, leads to arbitrariness and oppression. The concepts of economic interest and particular will become part of a method for undermining the moral individualism of Rousseau, to be replaced with a statist mentality. The state represents the rational will; the clue to individual rationality lies in conformity to the state which Hegel glorified.

Rousseau had envisaged a society with a great deal of participation; he had in mind the idea that liberty was only meaningful in the polis. Hegel reversed this expectation of activity; conformity to the state supplanted the norm of participation. Once it has been so defined and individualism has been undermined, the state can march on an independent course; the glory of the individual was to be found in the glory of the state.

That is hardly the end of the matter, for according to Hegelian theory history is the milieu of the state; its unfolding is that of the state. Reason as a concept justifies the state, and finds an analogue in history as the manifestation of reason. For Hegel the state is the vehicle by which historical development proceeds. Reason now differs from that of the Enlightenment; Hegel proposed the relativity of speculation. If what men think at any point takes place in relation to historical reason, which is constantly unfolding, what happens to the search for immutable law? Men at no stage can find universal laws, and all claims to abstract knowledge are damaged. Men reflect reason but they do not have it; they mirror truth without knowing it. Human beings become pawns of ideas that are developing. Thought is obsolete once it appears; as soon as it is conceived a larger idea is overleaping a current conception. That is why Hegel said that the owl of Minerva takes her flight at the fall of dusk. Philosophy comes too late genuinely to teach people what the world should be.

Hegel's mechanism for interpreting the historical process was the dialectical method, which was more elaborate a concept than any we have encountered so far. His historicist approach meant a considerable increase in the proposed apparatus. History proceeds by a divine purpose which men cannot really understand. The dialectic was a form of historical logic devised to comprehend the dynamic nature of change; it encompassed contradictions. In an age of great upheavals Hegel's dialectic was a technique for comprehending it in terms of logic. A thesis produces an antithesis that in turn becomes a synthesis; B emerges to counter A which leads to C, which Hegel saw as a higher manifestation of ultimate reason. For him the modern state was the ideal synthesis; the Greek world, followed and challenged by feudalism, produced Hegel's Prussia as the last word of reason. But the existence of the Prussian state does not prove it to be morally superior. Ethical ideals need not emerge out of conflict. But Hegel could not live by his own theories any more than the rest of the Reaction could. For why should history have stopped with Prussia?

Hegel's dialectic is closely related to some of our big questions. It was a logical formulation of dynamic historical changes as well as a union of norm and fact. This synthesis was not merely a large physical entity but always reflects the fact that reason is a moral fact. It is true that there is interaction everywhere. Hegel thought this idea comprehended history's dynamic quality, and he so structured his theory that it developed ever onward on a moral plane. But such scheduled progress meant a flight from responsibility, an attempt to shatter the tension between norms and reality while avoiding the problem of implementation. For Hegel men become the instruments of a process of ethical embodiment.

By this means the natural law proposition got reincorporated in the dialectic. The search for immutable law was undermined yet the mechanism of the dialectic, which established relativity, becomes the source of the fusion of norm and fact; the individual disappears in the process.

What is the way out? Karl Popper, in his concept of the "open society" and his critique of historicism, repudiates Hegel's procedure. In truth history can have no moral meaning; it is ethically meaningless. Ideal purposes reside only in participants; history has no predetermined goals. Ethics can be found in history, but moral values do not judge history independently of human choices. History is the storehouse of a thousand ethical systems; one can invoke a Christian evaluation of the events of 1789, but this operation has to be morally imposed even though Christianity is itself derived from history. The past presents us with ethical alternatives, yet any act of evaluation is an independent decision.

History is not its own judge and carries no ethical values. Therefore the problem of engineering a norm into history becomes crucial. The tension between history and the individual working normatively ought not to be obliterated. History is a social fact to be dealt with creatively; it is a limiting, coercive force but something to be manipulated, not a self-implementing drama about which an ethical chorus develops. Hegel's historical theory yielded highly poetic insights. He had the greatest historical sense; his theme of time was a source of special perception. The question of obsolescence, and what all these changes could mean, made Hegel the best representative of these essentially intuitive concerns.

14

A Free Society and Its Relation to the State

The Reaction held that the source of real slavery lies in a degraded self, and that society should become the instrument for overcoming this enslavement. Conservatives called the freedom of the Enlightenment coercion, and identified liberty with the controls of society. The social order was brought forward by means of the technique of eliminating the problem of emancipation as it was seen by the philosophes. But in this way the Reaction rendered freedom a meaningless concept. Assuming that we do not want to accept either the view of Rousseau or of the traditionalists, in both of which liberty becomes equivalent to social coercion, we must return to the Enlightenment conviction that freedom involves an absence of external restraint. Still we must acknowledge the impact of society on the individual.

Freedom can be understood to involve the capacity to alter and to change, the process of substituting social forms one for the other. In discussing Burke's insights into organizational coercions we introduced the principle of plural alternatives, and this idea can assume even larger dimensions. The power to change mythology as well as inherited traditions becomes critical. To abolish any of these tyrannies is impossible; yet to accept those that exist is unnecessary.

It is obligatory to abandon the Enlightenment's absolutist conception of freedom, even if it appears to set us adrift on a sea of essential relativism. Liberty ceases to be a goal to be won but becomes an unending quest. There can be no change that will not lead to the need for further alterations. It is a ceaseless battle, and one may always be returning to the same spot. As

Blaise Pascal wrote, "Man cannot sit still"; the principle that men do not sit still was missed by the Reaction. Freedom involves an unremitting struggle. The need for a permanent result, a "war to end all wars" for example, is an outgrowth of a characteristic failure of liberalism. The upshot is bound to be disillusionment with liberal experience. Its psychology, marked by optimism and gloom, has a manic-depressive quality. The Enlightenment's absolutism of orientation, and the consequent disenchantment, is a sign of social immaturity. Defining goals unrealistically is one means of escape from the problem.

The Enlightenment was basically correct in asserting the primacy of freedom; they looked on society as something the individual was getting away from, as opposed to trying to make him good. Freedom is a private value and in some sense means doing as one pleases. It is necessary to view coercions as an enemy. A red traffic light does not inspire any feeling of liberation and restraint is no clue to freedom. For liberty does not involve conformity to a moral law; becoming righteous is different from being free.

If you look at freedom in terms of emancipation from external restrictions, you have to concede that relatively small areas are open to manipulation. Even that most powerful election, the free choice of our individuality in life, is dependent on how our personality gets formed in the early family setting. Bonald's triad of father, mother, and child is telling here. Since man will never be able to conquer the whole range of social coercion, the area of liberty will be forever slight. But why should the problem of freedom arise at all? If individuals are so successfully shaped, why do not they just sit still?

The answer lies in the complexity of determinism itself, for it produces a multiplicity of influences. The impact of society is never wholly monolithic, which creates the problem of freedom. Bonald never saw this point; the triads do not necessarily go in the same direction. There can never be perfect harmony between mother and father in the raising of a child. The natural discord of parents is one basis for the plural determinants that confront us with the necessity of choice. Multiple forces drive an individual in conflicting directions. Therefore we necessarily become a judge, an evaluator, a decider; the germs for the search for freedom appear in the nature of the social order.

The notion that such a plural society is a good one must be based on some transcendent insight into the worth of the individual. It is never possible to establish empirically the value of such choice. The judgment in favor of individuality transcends the fact of the matter. One can defend individual freedom as an ethical insight; it is necessary to say this in order to assume the responsibility for achieving one's objective. We should avoid the confusion of both the Reaction and the Enlightenment and not take flight from the difficulty of implementing ideals. The inevitability of tension is the crux of the problem; the factual world never fully reflects ethical principles, and man must hold values in a world of fact because he cannot sit still. There is no avoiding this dilemma.

A more painful view of the world is implied in the recognition that the ideal of individuality is not guaranteed. We are left with the creative problem of engineering any ideal into reality. This is a far more activist view than that of the eighteenth century, or of Hegel's notion of the "liberation of the will." Men fight for one thing at a time as the forms of frustration shift; where one is stymied, one should act. The engineer is now the hero. The inability of the fact/value distinction to resolve itself into a unity means that we are left with the task of implementing goals. It should be possible in some measure to shape necessity.

Rousseau's concept of the legislator meant he was supposed to create something. The ancient Greek tradition proposed the possibility of bringing into existence the right thing in a hostile world. But this school of thought suggested that after such a creative act had been completed, institutions would carry on for good. We must instead envisage a legislator as a permanent figure involved in endless construction and reconstruction. History is no carrier of any inevitable solutions. It becomes nothing more than a brute social fact; old patterns are always alive. Creative will needs to be exercised; history is something we always have to deal with; it is an aspect of the coercive world that we seek to manipulate. History is not the embodiment of value, and no society that we cherish is bound to come into being. Existence is not ethically a determining factor; it does not achieve a value, nor undermine it; neither form of historicism is legitimate. As Popper has emphasized, history has no normative meaning. Society neither inevitably produces morality nor is it a destroyer of values.

This view is adjusted to the real dilemmas of existence; it takes into account the problem of liberty and the ultimate issue of method. There was an unreal character to all these philosophies; basically their otherworldliness stemmed from the effort to escape from painful problems. This fresh conception of freedom is not necessarily agreeable; it is indeterminate when it comes to achieving goals or winning or losing historically. The effort to escape unpleasantness accounts for the false treatments of freedom of both the Reaction and the Enlightenment.

The idea of free plurality involves a range of possibilities not always present, for there will be places where life will be miserable and where no alternative organizations are available. How can the ideal of alternatives be implemented in a compulsory organization like the state? Changing one's state is pretty difficult. A secondary principle comes in here: democracy. It is the only technique whereby the principle of alternatives can be instituted in a compulsory situation.

Montesquieu's view of political pluralism involved a system of checks and balances, which is not really the same as developing the choices that exist in a modern party system. Reciprocal checking means institutional pluralism but not the presence of alternatives. Montesquieu's proposal was a constitutional one but not democratic. And even his limited pluralism did not catch on in the eighteenth century.

We need to be able to change political regimes by relying on organizations that exist within the state. Political democracy is that technique for implementing alternatives within a compulsory context. The Enlightenment thinkers with their absolutes never touched on this problem. Rousseau's solution meant that no delegation of sovereignty was possible. He repudiated representation and therefore evolved no system whereby an exchange of regimes could be legitimate. We will be exploring the relation of the democratic state to the pursuit of the ideal of alternatives within society.

The Reaction did not win in spite of its valid societal insight. The conservatives failed to triumph historically on the basis of their good point. The social question could still be evaded and the Reaction ended up collapsing as a movement. In France, 1830 became a new phase of the French Revolution; in England, there was the Reform Act of 1832. A new burst of liberalism and its kind of thinking took place, even though there had been no real reply to the basic societal argument of the Reaction. We will want to inquire if liberalism in its mid-nineteenth-century form revised the outlook of the philosophes in such a way as to absorb the valid insight of the Reaction. The issue is whether nineteenth-century liberals tried to make realistic the Enlightenment ideal of individualism; it also raises the problem of whether it is possible for arguments to be left unanswered even though they are devastating. Our dominant question may become, does history have to bear any relation to conceptual analysis?

Part III

LIBERALISM

15

The Problem of Industrial Society

Three stages in the development of modern economics can be isolated: first the handicraft stage, which covers the corporate life of the eighteenth century; then the system of mercantile capitalism; and finally industrialism. Important social consequences accompanied these shifts in stages. New groups of mercantile capitalists and then industrial leaders developed. The rich merchant did not always become a wealthy industrialist. These changes inevitably had consequences on the structure of social life. Each of these broad factors was interconnected with the lives of individuals; the worker, instead of being involved in handicrafts, in the second stage needed merchants to market his goods; the wider the territory the more dependent the worker was on the merchant as a middleman. As industrialization proceeded the dependency increased. Urbanization in England therefore produced a new complexity in social life. Machinery involved large capital expenditures. In the handicraft stage the worker could possess his personal tools in his own shop; now the laborer had to enter the factory and sell his labor power.

Social interdependence as the market expanded was not uniquely related to the mercantile mode of production, for under industrialism the worker was caught up in the whole factory system. Nothing then could be produced without machines. The kind of discipline imposed by the industrial stage was immortalized by Adam Smith's discussion of the system involved in a pin factory; tightly organized control and division of labor were now necessities.

The privacy and individualism of the handicraft stage were inevitably lost. It takes more control just to get twenty people together. A kind of anarchy was possible under the handicraft scheme of production; however, capitalism's collective discipline meant that everyone must work. Moses Brown is a symbol of this new coercive structure in nineteenth-century New England. The mere fact of getting workers in the same room increased production, but the factory system involved the restraint of a special social system as well as that of the machine. Machinery sets the pace of production. A new kind of coercion had been produced, with the power to eliminate the self-will and intractability of individuals.

Friedrich Engels made this point about the socialization of the worker. The rise of towns and industrialization produced an integrated system. Industrial production is a social matter, which is why Marx discussed collective labor. There was a collectivization of the whole process of production. Capitalism socializes life, destroying the anarchy and independence of the earlier productive process. Marx proposed that it was the task of socialism to rationalize the collectivism of capitalism.

A decline in status on the part of the worker accompanied this increasing socialization. A shoemaker will have little social status in corporate society; yet he retained a sense of superiority when he was a producer with special skills. The sense of producer status remains with the workman in and through any discrimination. But in a factory system the worker may merely produce one item in the complicated production of shoes. He therefore loses, by collectivization, his earlier special standing. Socialization shattered the individual producer status of a workman rather than created a new category of equal social significance.

Capitalism produced both the middle class and the proletariat. What is the eye of the new working class focused on? It is not until late in the nineteenth century that it pursues an independent course. But its attention will inevitably concentrate on society; as a product of the new social system introduced under the banner of liberalism, it experienced the falsity of liberal theory. It underwent an increase of coercion as well as a loss of status; the inadequacy of the eighteenth-century formula, the atomism and the elimination of society, affected the working class most. The utopianism and unreality of the Enlightenment inspired the proletariat to reflect on the elimination of the social question by liberal thought. We now have a historical force interested in our own theoretical problem.

As an outgrowth of industrial society the new movement of liberal thought will not associate itself with the working class. The years 1830–48 are a period of peaceful and happy bourgeois supremacy in which the middle class itself basically reaffirms the eighteenth-century dream. This new manifestation of the bourgeois spirit was not in the same position as the philosophes, or even the middle class after the French Revolution. It faced not Wellington and Charles X but also on the Left the new proletarian groups that industrial society had brought into being. The forces below constituted a fresh dimension.

The middle class having to face both the Right and the Left paralleled the convolutions of the old feudal order after the French Revolution. The position of the middle class in this triangle meant that it could be crushed. But it was not to be true of the nineteenth-century liberals, whose political genius was to play both sides against the other by dividing and conquering. In the July Revolution of 1830 in France, the Reform Act of 1832 in England, and the European turmoil of 1848, liberalism used working class groups, hurling them against the old aristocratic order. The proletariat's aspirations were irrevocably democratic; they could not be taken in by reactionary corporatism. Basically, in this period the upper and lower classes did not ally against the middle class. The bourgeoisie was not afraid to appeal to the old order in order to control the Left, even though its peculiar dualism of mood often looked like simple hypocrisy. The liberals, in opposing the landed class, produced the laborer's own sense of class; but the liberals, when frightened of the proletariat they had brought into being, excluded them from such gains as came from either the advantages of the Reform Act or the expanded suffrage qualifications after the July Revolution. The middle class could be liberal and conservative at the same time, which helped inspire the motto, get as much as you can.

The English strand of utilitarian liberalism started with Bentham's *Fragment on Government*. He launched an attack on natural law in behalf of utility. Industrial capitalism, relatively highly developed in Britain, bore a special relation to the triumph of utilitarianism. Veblen stressed the contrast between the animistic outlook (similar to Comte's pre-positive theology) which saw things as supernatural, and then matter-of-fact modes of thought. Earlier natural law, functioning as a form of rationalism, corroded many of the most treasured mythologies of the old society. But natural law thinking was a stage in the development from animism to a down-to-earth viewpoint. Its norms were not associated with any existing society.

The growth of industrialization inspired a quantitative spirit. Natural law thinking still contained an animism that was at odds with the technology of industrial experience. There is an inherent contrast between applied science, which is a crucial aspect of industrialism, and the abstractness of natural law. Veblen saw that utility was more in tune with the industrial revolution than natural law. The utilitarian approach seeks to quantify morality into units of pleasure and pain that can be added and subtracted. Bentham wanted buckets of pleasure and pain that could be weighed and stacked as if in a balance sheet. Utilitarianism implied the possibility of quantifying moral problems.

The growth of utilitarianism in England was therefore a critical reflection of the industrial ethos. By the time of the liberal reliance in England on the standard of utility, the concept of natural law had lost its Voltairian meaning and had acquired Burkean overtones; Bentham objected to Blackstone's use of natural law in history on the grounds that it rationalized the status quo. When Bentham called natural rights "nonsense on stilts" it was already outmoded by the standards of English liberals. In trying to reform things, liberals needed a sociological jurisprudence like utilitarianism to examine actual institutions and to look at who stood to benefit from them. Natural law was by then identified with the defense of privilege. The capitalist environment had produced an industrial sort of morality; the reactionary reliance on natural law principles evoked a sociologically realistic analysis of institutions, as Bentham sought to puncture pretentious ways of supporting received authority.

Bentham's effort to quantify morality was not, however, very successful, since ethics cannot easily be industrialized. He attacked natural law on the grounds that everyone could interpret it as he pleases; Bentham wanted a more objective standard. Pleasures are in some sense measurable and capable of being added together. But ultimately pleasure was no less anarchical a principle. There are changing evaluations of pleasure, if only in terms of the contrast between the future and the present; one can use prices, that provide good quantification, but this was not Bentham's point. He wanted to be able to quantify how good it felt to experience different things.

Technical problems arise even in connection with the idea of establishing that each individual must count for one; ultimately it is an a priori concept that can not empirically be demonstrated. How can any form of egalitarianism be defended, given the differing capacities for the enjoyment of pleasure and pain? To Bentham's credit, though, he had erected a goal that could be used as an ideal fiction. There has always been some market mechanism functioning in our behavior toward pleasure; if one has a limited quantity of money one chooses between different alternatives. We do make decisions on the basis of some such calculations. The Benthamite scheme of industrialized morality, whatever its inadequacies, will have a permanent human relevance.

16

Bentham's Utilitarianism

Bentham defined the goal of the state broadly as that of maximizing happiness by erecting penalties to guide self-interest. But when it comes to how the state should be organized, Benthamite theory eventually shifted from an early belief in enlightened despotism to the later advocacy of democracy. He was both a representative of eighteenth-century Enlightenment doctrine as well as an apostle of early nineteenth-century liberalism. He first had believed in the need for an absolute despot who proceeded rationally. However, he began to apply his own philosophy to his failure at achieving reform; he thought his advice had been rejected because of the rulers' egotism. Instead of enlightened despotism he proposed to entrust the mission of public happiness, the greatest good of the greatest number, to the greatest mass of the people.

Bentham then thought that the free society could only be implemented by a free state. Utilitarianism represented a broadening of the perspective of liberalism. The democratic state was a solution to the problem of establishing alternatives in a compulsory organization. Democracy could be used for bringing about freedom. The shift in Bentham from absolutism to democracy represented an advance in the evolution of liberal thought. Elections as a technique for achieving choice meant a heightened maturity in liberalism.

Bentham should have had to confront the argument of Rousseau about the desirability of a small community in which delegation is not relied upon. If we want a parliamentary state, we must face up to Rousseau's doctrine that democracy is applicable only to a community in which authority is not delegated. Furthermore, Bentham should also have had to come to terms with the point of conservative theory about the sheer irrationality of human beings. The Reaction implied that the behavior of the public could not be relied upon; the stress on mass irrationality was an extension of the concept that personal evil requires external coercion.

The quest for a free society had become a search for a free state. Yet Bentham's work contained a considerable carry-over from eighteenth-century elitism; the government of men was held to be a specialized job along the lines of Adam Smith's notion of division of labor. The influence of the industrial revolution on Bentham can easily be seen.

Despite the influence of Enlightenment elitism, Bentham managed to establish a theory of democracy. His argument proceeded by a few basic steps. He began first with the principle that governors are separate from the mass of the people. Secondly, he thought that these rulers are egotistic, which complicates the problem; his disciple James Mill in his "Essay On Government" argued that the motivation of governors was almost sadistic, and that they will most ruthlessly exploit the people. The utilitarian formula for this impasse was to take the self-interest of the rulers, which appears as an absolute antithesis to the self-interest of the mass, and fuse the two by resolving them into a harmony. The means of identifying the rulers with the ruled was by the device of the principle of election and reelection.

According to utilitarian doctrine, democracy means that the people have the power periodically to throw governors out of office. This conception of democracy has the premise, therefore, that the supreme motivation of rulers, as in Hobbes's view of human nature, will be survival; the passion for self-aggrandizement will be redefined so that governors must satisfy the governed. In this way Benthamite thinking made the principle of self-interest the basis of parliamentary organization.

The utilitarian theory of representation still leaves us with unresolved questions. It did not answer Maistre and the conservatives who believed that people are so irrational that they cannot govern themselves; the Reaction had held that human nature was so evil that it had need of external control. Instead, Bentham assumes the rationality of people in the pursuit of their self-interest. But may they not be subject to waves of enthusiasm? The battle of liberals and elitist irrationalists today hinges on this matter. The liberals could then simply ignore the argument of conservatives but now they cannot; Maistre and Bonald have had their descendant in Robert Michels.

Bentham did overestimate the rationality of people. Little empirical evidence exists for assuming a certain economy between the choice of means that are appropriate to given ends. The issue is not whether people are as rational as Bentham thought, but whether they are rational enough to make the principle of representation have validity. There are limits to the lack of economy employed by the mass of the people; propaganda and bamboozlement do exist, yet there are boundaries to its extent. The matter becomes one of weighing the degree of rationality that the public has.

Bentham's belief that men can be free when being governed by representatives still has to counter Rousseau's contention that the English are only free at election times. Michels will argue that representatives gain power by an "iron law of oligarchy." But Bentham did not define freedom as being governed by elected men, but rather in terms of the electoral capacity to dislocate the government. Freedom lies in the power of exchange—not in the principle of representation. The capacity to reelect or to unelect governments became the key. In this capacity to exchange, Bentham saw something that Rousseau did not appreciate at all: the continuous result of that power of election over the life of representatives.

The question of social freedom is illuminated by the idea that alternatives open to an individual should be viewed in terms of the possibility of altering the types of coercions faced. Representative A, for example, constantly worries about the pro-Israeli vote which is important for his reelection. Similarly, if a worker can move between factories A and B, that chance of movement, like the possibility of reelection and unelection, must continue to live at all times. Threat of the possibility of dislocation in politics is a Benthamite contribution to liberalism. The principle of social demand, in which every institution expects the support of its workers, means there is always the danger that an organization will disappear if people desert it. As long as it is not a monopolistic situation the threat of withdrawal of support in the social sphere is as real as in the political one.

The consequences of implementing the Benthamite liberal goal are that when alternatives are created individuals are not only given freedom of movement, but such choices condition the behavior of organizations who are dependent on popular support. The mechanism of parliamentary government dependent on a broad suffrage was not yet established in the early nineteenth century; but we can see that one of the distinctive characteristics of this outburst of liberalism was the effort to create the machinery of the democratic state. Bentham had some sharp insights.

I have already discussed the psychological impact of the industrial revolution as well as the role of the middle class surrounded by different social pressures. The bourgeoisie instinctively feared the masses. The middle class nonetheless had to entertain Benthamite theory; there was a drive in the democratic direction. Having given up its earlier reliance on the monarchy it faced an alliance with the mass of people to accomplish its objectives. The drift toward democracy was inevitable for the middle class; Bentham relied on enlightened monarchy until it failed to appear. It turned out to be impossible to accomplish the bourgeoisie's goals unless the electorate was broadened.

The English liberals in fact linked the theory of democracy with middle-class rule. James Mill thought it would govern by determining social norms. The middle class was supposedly naturally superior to the lower class; they would psychologically dominate their social inferiors. Even if the lower class were given the vote there would be no upheaval in the norms of the middle class. Aristotle's own special enthusiasm for the middle class became the belief that its norms will permeate the rest of society. It was a ridiculous doctrine, yet in Victorian England middle-class norms did penetrate both upper and lower classes. But looking back, after the rise of socialism it was politically ludicrous to expect that it should continue to be so.

Most liberals in England in fact refused to accept the notion of democracy, and Thomas B. Macaulay was one of them. The Reform Act of 1832 only enfranchised the middle class. The argument of the liberals was that this was the last extension of the suffrage, and that the mass electorate would never really be introduced. Benthamism turns out not to be a key to English liberalism; the philosophy of the Reform Act was not theirs but that of the conservative Whigs. The important movements in British political thought having the power to reform were non-conformist religions such as Wesleyanism. Such ideas were not advanced in the spirit of Bentham, who was a secular theorist. One of the ironies, and virtues, of British history was that secular rationalism could be united with evangelical religions in behalf of reform.

Benthamite theory represents a great step forward with its theory of representation. But if Bentham made this notable political advance, he failed also to make a social one: he did not apply his political insights to the new social world of industrialism. The factory manager was not exchanged by any annual elections, nor was he subject to the same corrosive analysis of power that Bentham applies politically.

In Bentham's proposed role for the political sovereign in maximizing happiness one would think that there was a very positive notion; Owen will later take this concept and make it the basis of a socialist philosophy. The apparent affirmative social drift in Bentham's outlook was multiplied by the definition of ways of attaining the utilitarian goal; subsistence, abundance, equality, and security were all to be provided by the state. Yet Bentham's state at the same time did not have to do much; the government's responsibility was taken over by an assumed automatic social harmony. For abundance he relied on classical economic doctrine; subsistence was taken care of by the drive for survival, and equality was less important than security, which meant that property cannot be invaded.

The social sphere therefore remained fairly untouched by Bentham. He did not attempt to apply his political realism with respect to power in the social realm. He seized on the political aspect and developed the argument completely realistically. But he left the surrounding atomistic social world, first hypothesized by the philosophes, untouched. An unreal world still existed for him to the extent that the supposedly coercionless sphere of free contract remained unexamined.

The role of the state for Bentham was much like that of the Enlightenment's absolutism. The democratic state had been fortified, but he thought of the political task as that of only imposing penalties; this was in line with Hobbes's idea of providing "hedges" around which people move. The utilitarian mission in politics was not essentially constructive but a passive one. The state was to operate in cases of disrepair and breakdown.

An acutely democratized view of the Enlightenment still did not touch the essential eighteenth-century evasion of society. This avoidance of social reality could not endure forever. The introduction of the masses of the people to political power was full of implications for the future highlighting of society in political theory. This democracy was not going to be a neutral body; if Bentham was not concerned with the social world, democracy was. This was the fatal contradiction within Benthamite theory; the mass of people were focused on the problem of society.

17

John Stuart Mill

Bentham's tremendous ingenuity in the construction of a free state was not matched by the development of a strictly social theory. In politics he succeeded in introducing the idea of implementing choice by means of representation. Yet when it came to society, utilitarianism did not apply the principle of alternatives in an institutional way.

John Stuart Mill's thought represents a deepening of the Benthamite tradition as well as a shift in direction. For example, Mill feared the tyranny of the majority while early utilitarian thinking had been promajoritarian. If individuals could be reduced to equal units then the greatest happiness was supposed to be revealed in the largest majority. The problem of protecting minorities was hardly dealt with. The utilitarians assumed that because of the rationality of the majority it would not be in its interest to destroy minorities. The premise was a harmonious relation of interests between majority and minority. In behalf of its strategic orientation, which was to eliminate the grip of the old landed interests, utilitarian liberalism was promajoritarian.

By the time of Mill the old oligarchy had been overthrown. The question of the protection of minorities rather than the tyranny of an elite then seemed significant. But the majority Mill worries about is a different entity from what one might think—not a simple mathematical sum; a disembodied entity cannot be terrifying. Mill's majority is more vital and alive because it is a psychological force. He speaks in the mood of Tocqueville who feared that in the impact of the mass all intelligent variety is lost. The majority, in the form of mass opinion, becomes an oppressive instrument for the shaping of minds.

Such a majority can prevent the problem of individuality entirely by stifling the multiplicity out of which it springs. Mill touches on the psychological matrix from which behavior arises. There is a critical distinction between X politically defying Y and Z, and that wholly different situation where the psychological impact of Y and Z is so great that X does not even think of defiance.

Yet in discussing mass opinion Mill has exposed a reason why democracy was able to function at all. The Industrial Revolution succeeded in inspiring a great enhancement of the uniformity in life; the commodities on the assembly line are only one illustration. Industrial conformity also produces a certain degree of psychological uniformity, a shattering of variety in culture and the production of a new level of standardization.

To have democracy at all there must be a certain such uniformity of mass opinion. Thanks to the agitations of 1831 and 1832 a new political awareness spread over the British nation. Without the growth of such a mass consciousness it is hard to see how the modern state projected over a larger area could possibly work. Rousseau, living in a preindustrial time, considered it inconceivable that political consciousness could be extended beyond the city-state. The development of social and industrial techniques for the manufacture of public opinion over large areas disproved Rousseau's fears. The possibility that we can revert to Rousseau and do without representation and only have direct government is not tenable. The first paradox in John Stuart Mill's thought, then, is that the psychological majoritarianism he feared was the very foundation of the democracy he wanted.

The second paradox comes up also in his essay *On Liberty*. In fighting the tyranny of the majority one can distinguish between its psychological and political facets. For him the battle for psychological and political individualism meant that both of these struggles were united. But these two logically distinct aspects of the same concept represent incompatible positions, for to have political and civil liberty a certain degree of psychological conformity is necessary. When opinion is radically broken down into basic divisions, and the force of instinctive coercion has disintegrated, differences over the ultimate norms of society break out and political liberty is impossible; a state of anarchy then exists, which is likely to elicit the action of a politically despotic force.

Underlying political freedom then must be a certain amount of psychological uniformity. Civil liberty, though it seems to be the ally of nonconformism, is in many respects the product of an agreed-upon consensus. According to a superficial line of reasoning it is impossible to defend political liberty and social nonconformity as absolutes; but the real point is that no political system can bear the burden of civil liberty without a high degree of uniformity. Lord Balfour thought that Englishmen could safely afford to bicker because they had nothing special to argue about, and precisely because we know we are all good Americans we let Americans do relatively as they like. Two underlying contradictions, then, coexisted in Mill's thought.

Public opinion in the modern era is a constructive force organizing society and making it possible. A real problem comes with the blocking of spontaneity that Erich Fromm has written about. David Riesman, working in the tradition of Mill, Tocqueville, and Fromm, also objects to the standardization of men. Ernest Hemingway, in *For Whom the Bell Tolls,* presented Robert Jordan as an isolated individual sleeping out-of-doors in Spain; yet however romantically idiosyncratic the setting, Jordan dreamt of the Hollywood star Jean Harlow. She was a standardized and uniformly available symbol; in the modern world, public and private areas of life begin to dissolve.

Such standardization involves manipulation; there is an element of manufacture in symbols. The manipulative quality in public symbols constitutes a danger to democracy, yet it is indispensable to the production of public opinion. The threat arises out of the very materials of democracy itself. Mass opinion is destructive of psychological plurality, opening the way to a new elitist manipulative aspect; yet, although he attacked the evils of conformity, it appears that that uniformity springs from the parliamentary system to which Mill was devoted.

Mill's solution was to retreat from the democracy as developed earlier by Bentham. According to Burke the individual representative should be free to choose his own course of action, and Mill also advocated the power of plural voting for the educated elite in order to keep mass opinion in its place. Mere mechanical devices were no real solution to the issue he raises. He could not see in society a force to resist the trend toward conformity. He wanted to fight back against uniformity, but that was as far as he got.

Mill saw the majority as a live social force and not just as a numerical matter. The psychological coercions stemming from the uniformity of bourgeois society made the situation in pre-revolutionary society look by contrast rich in local variety. Mill's dilemmas do not exist in old feudal society which was localized. A high degree of multiplicity prevailed in the ancien régime as a matter of course.

We can compare Burke and Mill on this count, for Burke's fear is precisely the idea that new liberal forces will reduce all things to uniformity. He glories in the diversity of corporate society; Mill's own lament links him to conservatism, and he locks hands with Burke on the issue of representation. Mill instinctively moves in the direction of the allies of the old corporate system.

On the issue of Mill's relationship with conservatism, he and the other romantics regretted that the variety and individuality of life was disappearing; he too stressed the unique and the individual. The romantics were concerned with the imponderable in reacting against the standardization of society. Maistre had emphasized that nations are different and that people are varied. Mill was heavily influenced by the romantic trend.

Mill is no conservative, however, and will not go back to the old regime; he wants individualism within the context of the new society. The tragedy of Mill was that he intended individualism to mean private and solitary experience; but the ideal of individualism had the purpose of producing a set of equal atoms which were separate and yet precisely similar. Individualism in its full sense requires diversity as well as isolation. In the elevation of Mill's norms a levelling takes place; an inherent tendency against diversity was apparent, and Mill could not face this fact.

It is a familiar dilemma, consistent with the rest of Mill's thought, that he was in a state of tension between individualism and socialism. He was not a resolved thinker, and his work was marked by an inability to come to terms with himself. His failure to arrive at a unified judgment may be due to the intrinsic complexity of the problem, or to his not wanting to resolve it. Intellectual honesty does not require ambivalence.

Private property was essential to Mill; one should not make too much of his attempts to dissolve vestiges of the ancien régime like primogeniture or the right of entail. The socialism that he advocated at the end of his life was not radical, and amounted to an acceptance of trade unions. He never had to sacrifice his basic tenets to accept such unionism.

Mill emerges as a liberal who goes beyond politics to society. He sensed that all was not well in the vast social sea. He felt the presence of social coercion, the psychological power that is a socially subterranean aspect of tyranny. The problem of society emerges in Mill. He sees coercions in the social world, at which point he sounds like Carlyle, Ruskin, Hegel, and Comte. Mill, together with these men, perceived that a real society existed.

Mill does not go back, however, to the old society; he was committed to the new one. He attempted to articulate an amorphous kind of socialism within the context of liberal ideals. He epitomizes the dilemma of a liberal who sees that a new social order has been created under the banner of liberalism, and harks back to the old regime; yet because of his commitment to liberalism he cannot accept the conservative solution.

A tension arose in the liberal movement from the problem of social liberty having been evaded since the mid-eighteenth century; yet it cannot work out a real solution to the problem in terms of the liberal idea. Mill was suspended between the reality of the old order and the fictions of the new; he was an English Rousseau but lacked Rousseau's courage. He was a more timid man than Rousseau, tortured and troubled by his perceptions.

According to the analysis of representation in early utilitarian thought, the advantage of rulers can be identified with the self-interest of the mass in order to produce a system of political peace. James Mill worked out this theory in his "Essay on Government." The device of elections was designed to make human badness equivalent to goodness. But if rulers were this bad, as self-interested as all this, the whole system would not work. The public would never get the system back, and a permanent elite would arise. In the functioning of society other factors limit the power of rulers than the fear of losing electorally; in *A System of Logic* Mill discusses points like the sense of duty, philanthropy, and cultural mores—all the traditions stemming from the past. Mill saw that these forces are psychological and, along with formal Benthamite checks, also at work. The shape of any American president's behavior, for example, has to be in conformity with traditions. The failure of parliamentary institutions to develop is not just because Benthamite gadgetry is not there, but also because the appropriate psychological forces are not present.

Here we have a third correlation with conservatism, for the concern with tradition and history turns Mill from the abstract rationalism of Benthamism. Mill was aware of history, diversity, and society. He attacks Bentham and John Austin as ahistorical. He, like Maistre, criticizes the notion that there is a universal man. In talking about national customs he is rediscovering the whole notion of tradition and manifests a concern with the actual functioning of a social system. He struggles with the question of freedom in a real society; he pursues the societal insight. Before he died in 1873 he saw that the harnessing of liberty to a social vacuum led to the creation of a new society with its own problems.

In his *System of Logic,* Mill moved on the methodological plane to assail two types: the chemical method made loose comparison unsound because one cannot experiment with society; and the abstract geometric method of the classical utilitarians and the Enlightenment was also unreliable. He speaks about Comte's metaphysical category under the heading of the geometric method. The question of social unreality was the point of departure for Mill's analysis of society. In fact, Comte heavily influenced Mill in the direction of the method of sociology; Mill criticizes the whole Enlightenment on the grounds of the absence of empiricism.

Method was Mill's starting point for social perception. To say that the Enlightenment lacked social empiricism was to invite the analysis of society. Mill could not tolerate Comte's solution, since Comte was willing to go back to the medieval arrangement of a priesthood. Mill was horrified at this idea, since he was committed to the liberal movement, and so he ended up with no solution of his own except the whole dilemma of the social problem. Mill had a set of disorganized perceptions. He was concerned with social freedom, economic individualism, and the power of history and tradition. English liberalism had come to recognize the emergence of the social problem; Mill leads in the direction of the idealist and feudal romantics but comes to no resolution himself.

18

Pierre-Paul Royer-Collard

Royer-Collard's philosophy was connected with the Charter of 1814. He was the seminal mind of the active political group known as the Doctrinaires. Their doctrine was an attempt to forge a middle ground between the "Ultras" like Bonald and the extreme radicals. He resembled Burke in that his work came out in speeches in behalf of the charter. But France had had a revolution while England did not; the shadow of the Revolution conditions everything in France, and its liberalism was an attempt to come to terms with 1789.

He was a constitutionalist determined to handle the concept of sovereignty by placing it in reason. There are crucial distinctions between how Bentham, Austin, and Rousseau handled sovereignty. In the traditional approach sovereign power is placed in some determinate political entity, either the people or a legislature. The idea that there are any norms beyond such a body that can determine its action would seem the very target against which sovereignty is directed. The concept represents an effort to try to discover the supreme source of power; when it is placed in a notion like reason its whole traditional meaning is destroyed, for it becomes impossible to discover any determinate body about which there cannot be controversy.

Liberal thought differed in France and England. Bentham and Austin were supporters of sovereignty, while Royer-Collard annihilated the concept. England in 1832 was embarking on a peculiar revolution of its own; the execution of earlier reforms had been arrested with the Reaction against the Revolution. In order to accomplish reform impulses, they needed a supreme power that had the force to dissolve old customary restrictions. But France had experienced its Revolution, and had plenty of experience with sovereignty and the uses of despotism for social reform. Liberals wished to recover from the impact of the Revolution and keep the demon in check.

The whole drift of French liberal thought had as its purpose keeping things under control. While utilitarian liberalism had rejected, along with the philosophes, the notion of checks and balances, Montesquieu now becomes an idol of French liberal thought; the idea of divided power established by placing sovereignty in reason was just what the Enlightenment had opposed. The Charter of 1814 embodied the monarchy, the Chamber of Deputies, and the Chamber of Peers in order to check each other; it was a denial of the search of unity of the English liberals and the French eighteenth-century political thinkers.

The French liberals did not justify these institutional powers because they represented numerical groups; the concept of representation through number leads to popular sovereignty. The French liberals substituted the eighteenth-century Whig idea instead of the one-man-one-vote notion of the English utilitarians. This Whig version had meant representation by interests. Monarchy, peers, and the populace are to have power simply because three big interests are in existence; they would represent the true social forces of the community. There is no need for complete popular representation; all the people do not have to possess the right to vote. This permitted Royer-Collard to justify the extraordinarily high property requirement for being an elector. Interest was a substitute for numbers. Instead of the principle of one man one vote, the upper bourgeoisie was to represent the whole interest. This approach permitted a limited suffrage.

The popular branch was to preserve the liberties of speech, press, and the right of a jury trial. The elite of peers (also accepted by François Guizot for the July Monarchy) represented the interest concerned with ancient glory. Since the rigid egalitarianism of Benthamism was excluded, it was therefore unnecessary to reconcile this liberal theory with the actual empirical dominion of the middle class. Nineteenth-century English liberals had to struggle with a conflict between egalitar-

ianism and the supremacy of the middle class. French liberals
do not have anything to reconcile, since they were defenders of
limited suffrage. The mood of Macaulay and Henry Peter
Brougham, who did not accept manhood suffrage, differed
from that of the French liberals. France had the memory of the
Revolution; in England the democratic impulse had not yet
been felt, and therefore the egalitarian doctrine was not feared.
French liberals sought to qualify democratic ideas and limit
power. They were in mood fearful and compromising; they lacked
the optimism of England and sought to forward nothing but to
qualify the experiences that already existed.

Royer-Collard did reflect on how society relates to the political system. According to him the government must correlate
itself with the structure underlying it. A state has to be geared
to the basic needs of society. We see here the influence of the
traditionalists. Royer-Collard was trying to think through the
problem of politics in a society that had been torn apart. There
was difficulty in discovering any political order to match a
society so wracked with conflict. The social situation was inherently explosive. A critical problem was the relation of the state
to society. The English could take this for granted since they
had a secure society. In France it was clearer that a stable
political order must be delicately constructed. Royer-Collard
was ready to institutionalize those political inequalities that
represented social diversities. The restricted suffrage and the
Chamber of Peers were justified because they were the political
parallel of social inequalities and necessary to achieve stability.

Royer-Collard also proposed that a political order, in and of
itself, has a symbolic weight. Over time it gains autonomous
moral and psychological force in society. The political so-called
superstructure attains autonomy. In his system of insights,
politics is reflexive of society but also develops the force to
contribute something to the outcome of events.

He spoke of the charter as if it were a religious document. He
wanted to make a popular fetish out of it, and promote a kind of
charter worship. He proposed having the political settlement
itself become the point of departure to heal the divisions of
society. This kind of constitution worship emerged spontaneously in the United States only because of the preceding una-

nimity of society; in America the Constitution has been a stabilizing factor, but in France there were tremendous moral and ultimate ethical divisions. It is hopeless to try to establish a worship of a charter that is repudiated in its underlying principles by half the population. Royer-Collard overlooked the need for a basic community that would provide the will to cooperate in spite of the possibility of intense competition.

We can agree that politics should be correlated to society. Yet his own proposed political set-up did not reflect the social forces in France. He gave the monarchy and nobility two-thirds of the power, although they were propped up on uneasy foundations. The bourgeoisie, as 1830 proved, required more power. The Chamber of Deputies was limited to the upper bourgeoisie, and therefore threatened politically by the rise of the petit bourgeoisie to increasing social power as well as by the emergence of the proletariat. Royer-Collard's system amounted to a massive repudiation of his own premises. Yet his philosophic impulse was to avert revolution; social forces without political power create the basis for a revolutionary situation.

To him the idea of mass representation was bad. First, the people had no experience in government; they owned too little property, and they were easily corrupted. Even if all this were true, he should have pursued his profound insight; it would then have been necessary to eliminate those evils not by exclusion from the system but by a salutary remedy. On his own grounds it was impossible to exclude a major interest because you do not like it or it is evil; it still must be included. His bias for the upper bourgeoisie and its alliance with the old social order was so great that it overrode the genuine insights of his thinking. These obvious objections could not have escaped him except for his own prejudices.

The Charter of 1814 turned out to be very unpopular. Social tensions, such as those between the upper and the lower bourgeoisie, undermined it. The whole structure of the situation was not conducive to an atmosphere of agreement surrounding the charter. Charles X intended to root out any compromises; he was institutionalizing a kind of civil war. An unsolved social conflict lay beneath the constitution. In the circumstances of a social war of interests, an attempt to create religious fetishism made no sense.

Like Mill, Royer-Collard had begun to see difficulties outside the political sphere—the social context of politics. Bentham had stood for an advance in institutional creativity. Mill had possessed insight into the social difficulties around liberal theories. Royer-Collard's concern for the social context was as keen as Mill's, but he did not resolve the basic conflict because he was inhibited, like Mill, by his liberal biases from coming to a conclusion.

These liberals were tortured spirits who sensed an immense problem that had been avoided, but they could not come to a fundamental resolution of the issue. Nineteenth-century liberalism in both France and England was optimistic and made great strides, yet there was a mood of impending catastrophe to their work.

Basically Royer-Collard had relied on the upper middle class in the Chamber of Deputies. The Enlightenment had justified its extreme egalitarianism by means of natural law and its rights—equality, reason, nature, etc. It was the application of these principles that brought in the proletariat and helped create it as a political force. When fighting against the ancien régime, liberals spoke of equality; they therefore rationalized the introduction of the lower classes into political power. Once the upper middle class had gone through the Revolution, they knew it was foolish to repeat the old rationale; they were frightened of the extreme egalitarianism in the utilitarian thinking in Britain. The Doctrinaires in France must now say what they mean, and make certain that destructive potentialities do not exist in its position. This accounts for Royer-Collard's complicated representational scheme.

The concept of reason for Royal-Collard and the Doctrinaires did not mean anything like the Enlightenment's natural order of equality proclaiming wide uniformity among people. It was not this kind of rationalism the liberals in France now had in mind. For Royer-Collard reason meant an approach that was manifested in checks and balances; he was concerned with distributive justice, the mean of Aristotle. The rational man compromises, and rationality lies in balance. A deeper justification of the middle class came in the concept of reason as the mean.

The ideal of the middle class as a mean between extremes was part of the unconscious Aristotelianism that arose in England as well as in France. The middle class became the bearer of reason. It had experience with management and was educated by revolution so that it was no longer turbulent. Yet this outlook contrasted with a true Aristotelian state, which was a mixed polity in which all groups had some power. Royer-Collard's theory was ready to exclude some groups in favor of the middle class. One can question how valid was this whole middle-class theory of politics. Is the middle class truly the basis of order, liberty, and freedom?

The nineteenth century was a dynamic age, while the era of the Athenian commonwealth was by comparison socially static. James Mill and Royer-Collard both advocated theories that were being projected into a new context when the middle class was being placed between two encroaching powers. It was not presiding over the other two forces but being squeezed by them. The supposed theoretical beauty of the middle class depends entirely on its context.

In modern times the aristocratic element had fallen out, and the middle class was caught between plutocracy and the proletariat. During the rise of fascism the middle class had a tendency to move hysterically to the Right. The function of the middle class depends wholly on its setting, so there is nothing especially good about the middle position.

The point that stability lies not in a class but in a whole society goes against Royer-Collard; it is achieved when the social and political systems relate to each other. Stability can be achieved through the middle class only if it is dominant socially. But Royer-Collard was committed to middle-class supremacy as an independent principle. When Marx said that the state was the executive agent of the middle class, he was not unmasking his opponents but saying exactly what they had earlier maintained, with a different value judgment to be sure.

In contrast to the approach of the philosophes—which in many ways Marx shared—for Royer-Collard, reason was defined as the mean between extremes. It does not determine substantive reality; the limits are given and taken to be nonrational. A certain empiricism was attached to this theory of rationalism; the boundaries are set by history. It involved an inescapable pragmatism. History gives the extremes, which include the Revolution; the task of rational man is to work within the historical inheritance. In contrast, Condorcet's rationalism aimed to dissolve the past. Royer-Collard proposed that rational man would tip-toe through the ruins of history.

Condorcet as a revolutionary was interested in sweeping away the past. A fundamental transformation in French liberal thought came about as a result of the Revolution. Liberalism aimed to surrender to circumstances, and not try to do too much. The optimism of the eighteenth century turns into this period's pessimism. One gets a peculiar mood on the part of the bourgeoisie that can be strategically accounted for; the French liberals sought to function in terms of forces they confronted, instead of reconstructing society.

19

Benjamin Constant

Bentham's philosophic contribution to the institution of parliamentary government was the theory of representation, which addressed the problem of alternatives in the compulsory sphere of the state; but he evaded the social question. For John Stuart Mill, such a simple-minded evasion could not be tolerated, but he was left with only liberal equipment and came up with no solution to a range of social issues. Royer-Collard had a comparable problem; he was unable to relate his political insight to the social picture. He was sensitive to social needs but remained without the will to come to grips with them. Both Mill and Royer-Collard lacked Bentham's optimism and their indecision was part of a gloomy inability to handle their problems.

Benjamin Constant stood to the Left of both Royer-Collard and Guizot; although Constant represented the Left, Guizot the Center, and Royer-Collard the Right, in philosophies they came down to the same thing. The petit bourgeoisie became a political force which was decisive in 1848 in overturning the July Monarchy. No large-scale liberal thought succeeded in emerging. Liberalism was caught between emergent socialism and the thinking of the upper bourgeoisie allied with the traditionalists. It never attained an independent destiny politically, and did not succeed in producing a coherent doctrine.

The whole concept of sovereignty was different in England and France. Bentham and Austin advocated an unlimited sovereign that harked back to the idea of the legislator and the Enlightenment's belief in benign despots. Royer-Collard embodied this concept in reason, and then nullified its empirical impact by means of proposing separation of powers and checks and balances. Popular sovereignty is itself no assurance of freedom; Rousseau's argument against representation was that since the people cannot act as one and must give power to delegates it leads inexorably to tyranny. Unlike Rousseau, Constant does not urge a small state but instead breaks up power within the state.

Bentham had answered Rousseau with his theory of alternative candidates and the power electorally to dislocate; he did so to destroy Rousseau's argument that representation means tyranny. Constant did not repudiate Bentham and became a chief contributor to theories about the mechanics of parliamentarism. According to Constant popular sovereignty must lie in the people, but be sharply bounded by the limits of individual rights and natural law. Yet the concept of sovereignty loses meaning when it is so restricted; it has to entail unlimited power. It was characteristic of Royer-Collard to surrender the concept to an abstraction. Locke wrote about power, but not without limits; he never used the concept of sovereignty.

Despite Constant's search for constitutionalism he was unwilling to give up the sovereignty idea that stood in its way. It was an integral part of the French tradition of political thought. Yet the memory of unlimited sovereignty was so bitter that the liberals tried to avoid the consequences of the idea. Constant accepted natural law and natural right, neither of which would be tolerable to Royer-Collard, who had a pragmatic Burkean outlook on reason as a mean between extremes. Constant adopted universalistic ideas as a means of limiting power, which brought him back to the world of the eighteenth century.

Still, Constant is a theorist of the separation of powers, and this plurality clashed with the Enlightenment's search for unity. He revived Montesquieu, and proposed there be four powers: royalty, a cabinet executive, two representative houses (hereditary and elected), and an independent judiciary. It amounted to a Rube Goldberg device. Constant remains in the tradition of Royer-Collard, timid and fearful of unlimited power.

Despite the protestations about democracy, the proposed elected chamber excluded the masses of the people; the elective branch had high property qualifications. Royer-Collard thought the public at large had no experience with management and were corruptible. Constant had no keen sense of building government on society; yet his plan was based on similar ideas to those of Royer-Collard, and Constant too failed to appreciate the movement within French society. He thought the masses do not have the leisure to engage in political activity; in contrast to Rousseau, Constant confined politics to a small class. Both Royer-Collard and Constant missed the emergence of the petit-bourgeois and the proletariat. The 1848 Revolution demonstrated that this system did not coincide with the emergent classes in the real society of France. The continuance of the master-image of the upper-middle class, like the English Whigs, was a European-wide phenomenon defending elite rule.

Constant's insights in politics and economics make an instructive comparison to the outlook of the Reaction. He had a peculiarly acute appreciation of the technique of parliamentary government; he defended the concept of a cabinet responsible to parliament. To have cabinet responsibility there must also be an organized opposition ready to take over; therefore a party system has to be developed. Constant saw the need for the continuing presence of two alternative entities that would compete for the immediate task of ruling the state. His reasoning also implied a common area of agreement so that the party system will not disrupt the whole basis of the parliamentary regime: a consensus on parliamentary procedure.

The functioning of this system also took for granted an underlying agreement about the values that the regime seems to further. Constant's contribution matches Bentham's inventiveness with his own insights. Constant supplemented the utilitarian theory of representation which was a formalistic scheme. In order to implement Bentham, there needs to be something like a parliamentary system, a cabinet, and parties, as well as underlying moral agreement. In writing about this realm of extra-legal institutions Constant made a very considerable contribution to the mechanics of parliamentary government. This was to be the fundamental achievement of mid-nineteenth-century liberalism. The net result was to make democracy feasible in a large community. By redefining political freedom in terms of the permanent existence of alternatives, and by making the threat of dislocation or alternation in governing elites realistic, a great advance was made over the simple popular sovereignty of Rousseau.

The utilitarians had failed because their theory remained political, not societal; they did not seek freedom for the individual in a real social setting. And a basic question about the French liberals remains: did Constant apply this ingenuity to the social sphere? He made no attempt to expand this concept about the development of freedom in the compulsory context of the state; he did not extend it to the realm of society. He says that freedom already exists in the economic sphere, and he repeats Adam Smith and J. B. Say. Constant did not even have the consciousness of the problem that can be found in John Stuart Mill and Royer-Collard. It looks like the more ingenious a thinker was in the construction of alternatives politically, the more blind he was to the social sphere.

Given Constant's own premises the two fields cannot be separated; if an underlying moral community is needed for parties to function, it does not come from the political realm alone. Such agreement is a social instinct; revolutions broke out in France because the political sphere got out of tune with society. Constant's view of parties, in which he urges the necessity of a basic ideological consensus, was dissociated from any examination of the social world. Royer-Collard's worship of the Charter of 1814 was similarly mistaken. Michels also made the point about the task of philosophy being exclusively political for the French liberals.

Constant's concern for ancient and modern liberty was not unique. The ancient city-state was totalitarian in that it controlled collectively all aspects of life; but it was also the home of freedom because of the degree of participation it allowed. In the modern state this type of liberty is impossible; Constant redefined it to mean the presence of basic limitations: freedom from state interference makes the individual's liberty inviolable. In contrast to the ancient world, states were now too large and complex, and there were no slaves; Constant disintegrated the image of liberty as achieved through participation. It was a reply to the totalitarian freedom of Rousseau who had quested for the old unity of the city-state. Rousseau had the polis in mind as well as the notion of unlimited popular sovereignty. In Constant's repudiating the Jacobin approach to liberty, he also rejected the ancient Greek ideal, and this decision was connected with the desire to dismiss the revolutionary experience. It was good that the idea of ancient liberty was finally put to rest by Constant.

But we cannot stop here. Rousseau rediscovered the polis when he did because he sought to legitimize the inherent coercion of the social world; he advocated the democratization and nationalization of coercions. Constant might have permanently settled the issue, but he merely states that liberty lies in free speech, freedom to trade, and an absence of coercions. Constant should have gone beyond this to the level of rejecting the Greek ideal of participant freedom. He should have resolved the issue of the need for the reappearance of the ideal which stems from an effort to make tolerable inescapable social coercions. Rousseau's solution is a powerful one: if you cannot get rid of social coercions, legitimize them by democratization.

Constant did not produce a solution to this need, together with his refutation of the Greek concept of freedom in modern times. His repudiation of Rousseau's idea proceeded politically and on a logical plane; he wrote about why men should have been so ridiculous as to have taken such a position. The concern with the polis concept is pervasive in modern political thought. Yet the underlying mechanism has not been studied; liberals were not interested enough in a solution to the social problem.

The Rousseauian urge will descend again and again in an attempt to deal with this unspoken recognition of society. Socialism will propose nationalization as a solution. Rousseau was being manufactured historically just as he was being destroyed philosophically. Socialism can be understood as an attempt to nationalize coercions, and through participation produce freedom. Where does the liberal inability to grapple with the problem of society come from? If it was a logical mistake, the error was in the context of its being repeatedly exposed by the arguments of the traditionalists. The compulsions of class meant liberals duplicated the societal mistake because those coercions operated in its interest. Blind spots can be attributed to a fundamental limitation on thinking by the class position of the theorists; they were compelled to duplicate the Enlightenment's own errors. But the question of class strategy alerts us that the proletariat had as its own purpose a concern with the social question. As with the philosophes it would be asking too much of the proletariat to create a new society as well as destroy it; we found it unfair to press any philosopher for such a comprehensive solution.

It is questionable how long a movement can continue with a scheme of thought representing a patent evasion of a critical problem like the social question. A group of thinkers can continue with such a fallacy for just so long. One never finds in liberalism an elaborate reply to the reactionary thinkers, as liberals repeat their own premises. They ignore the arguments of the Reaction and proceed with their own societal illusions. The evading of the reactionary position might well take place given the traditionalistic context of their thinking; they clothed a good idea in an obsolete world. They presented a valid social insight but within a medieval framework. Liberalism did not need to reply to the idea in such a form, since it represented discredited interests.

But a new force had begun to develop that cast the same idea in a new form. Liberalism in relation to socialism differs from its connection with conservatism, even though socialism and conservatism are united in their preoccupation with society. Liberalism can evade feudal socialism but it cannot avoid socialism itself. There are limits to how long this can go on. And these boundaries, if not set by intellectual issues, are determined by historical forces. There is a marked continuity of the Reaction and socialism concerning the social question. All these movements of thought need to be interpreted together. Mazzini had socialist tendencies and the transition from him to Fourier and Pierre J. Proudhon is logical. Yet one has to remember the significance of liberal political ingenuity, which remains the great liberal contribution in the nineteenth century.

20

Italy and Mazzini

Italy presents a special setting for understanding its political theorists. For it was still divided among other powers and lacking in national unity. Furthermore, the economy of commercial and industrial forces was backward, as Italy had missed the advance of capitalism. Nevertheless Mazzini crystallized the problems of other mid-nineteenth-century liberals and his work reflected the whole of European thinking. He is known as a nationalist theorist, which is true enough, but that label has distorted the full scope of his thought.

He was not a believer in solidaristic nationalism, but rather gloried in the free plurality of association, which it had been the mission of Rousseau to discredit. Associations in his view were crucial for the unfolding of the moral nature of man. He insisted that progress is made through minority associations, which express impulses of interest and principle, and therefore accomplish progressive action. In his view these free associations can challenge the power of the state itself. But Mazzini did not grasp that the liberty of the individual does not lie in his ability to form an association, but in his capacity to leave it. Mazzini left out the critical importance of the competitive factor, the way alternative associations may perform the same purposes. Mazzini, like Owen later, rejects the value of competition.

Mazzini did make a crucial distinction governing the relation of the state and associations; both are supreme in their proper areas. Those things that concern the group are separate from that which touches everyone. For Rousseau all of man's social

171

life concerned everyone; in his philosophy the drive for unity made the state the only legitimate source of coercion. In Mazzini we begin to find an analysis of the concept of free plurality which we have been evolving, although he assigns the state no special role in preserving the existence of a fluid variety of associations. But he does escape from the atomism of liberalism, as well as from Rousseau's solidaristic solution and the corporatist outlook of the Reaction.

One can question whether Mazzini's distinction between that which touches the group as opposed to that which concerns everyone can be tenable. It parallels John Stuart Mill's point about the difference between self-regarding and other-regarding concerns. Given the development of modern society it does seem that any one group has to influence everyone else. As society becomes increasingly complex Mazzini's distinction becomes harder to maintain. Yet some such principle has got, as a norm, to be maintained. The fact that the line becomes more difficult to establish does not mean that we should give it up, since it embodies a moral purpose.

In connection with the power of the association in relation to the individual members, Mazzini thought that no association can violate basic liberties. He also worked out a concept of the relationship of the association to the state: an association has an independent sphere from the state as an individual has separate autonomy from the association. He was advocating a theory of free plurality which was not liberal atomism, nor Rousseauian solidarity, and not stratified plurality. It has as its basis freedom and flexibility for the individual as well as for the association. Mazzini fills in rather abstractly that part of the social world outside the state that liberalism had left out.

We are partly misled about Mazzini because he is such a moralist. He reminds us of Rousseau and his particular solution. Mazzini levels a frontal attack on Bentham's utilitarian hedonism; Bentham omitted the spiritual world in which freedom must be constructed. Mazzini thought religion was the most important problem; he was concerned with the ethical side of man and the religious aspect of the issue. He was concentrating on duty; his primary concern was that liberties could not be viewed apart from duties. His notion of positive obligations reminds us of Rousseau and the rational will concept that arises in Comte and Hegelian idealism. Mazzini' s moralistic concern with positive freedom has obscured his contribution to the organizational question, for he was a pluralist and an individualist.

Unfortunately his special perception did not come from the beginnings of a new strand in liberalism. One of the influences on his mind when he spoke of free associations was a special Italian one: he was thinking of the clandestine *carbonari*. A Europeanwide experience with an underground political movement also existed; therefore, the crucial doctrinal influence for him did not come from within liberalism but represented an emergent strand of socialist thinking. The socialism of Owen and Fourier was based on a chain of associations and inspired Mazzini's preoccupations. This socialist theory arises to deal with the question of industrial community and the problem of the new feudalism. It suggests not that liberalism has come to deal with the social question but that liberalism has failed to confront it.

Mazzini did not accept Fourier's associationalism. He himself was proposing an abstract principle of free associational life without socialism. The phalanx was interpreted by him in liberal terms. Mazzini could not go along with Fourier because of the persistence of his liberal biases as well as his nationalism. Socialists were of course deeply antinationalistic. Mazzini's work is in these terms a confession of the collapse of liberalism and the triumph of socialism as the only movement that can come to grips with the social question. Mazzini was determined to remain both a moralist and a nationalist.

He lamented that democracy and liberalism had been separated from religion because of the loss of a proper sense of duty. Religion had become divorced from liberalism as in the secular, rationalistic spirit of utilitarianism. It was an atheistic philosophy in keeping with the intentions of the philosophes. The reform impulses of the early nineteenth century were various, however, and included evangelical religion and Christian reform movements. In France, liberals of the nineteenth century held to an old Catholicism out of a fear of the Revolution. The Doctrinaires like Guizot and Constant were philosophic defenders of the Church and not eighteenth-century secular liberals.

Mazzini's description of liberalism's isolation from religion was not quite accurate to begin with, yet there was a grain of truth to his indictment. Liberalism was linked with a secular impulse because of the social role that religion played in this period. Religion had become a conservative force. An established church existed in France, Italy, and England; each was instinctively connected to tendencies in the old society which liberalism sought to alter. Liberalism was inspired to become secular because of the strategic alignment of forces.

As religion became secularized liberalism became a religion itself. A millennial passion arose out of the psychological transfer from Christianity to liberalism of religious experience and its special emotions. In countries where nonconformism and evangelicalism could associate with progressive forces, the intensity of political philosophy in religious terms is lower than in places where this is not so. The sense of millennial upheaval did not arise in England in 1832 as it did in France in 1789 because in France the Church had become an instrument of the ancien régime; it was so deeply enmeshed with traditionalism that it symbolized the old order and provoked the tendency for religious passion to be transferred to political theory.

If the concept of salvation is reactionary we will get a liberal version of it in political terms. Tocqueville wrote about the Jacobins having transferred religion to political symbols. In England the development of evangelical religion made it possible to be both liberal and religious; they did not have to make a religion out of politics.

The American experience was one in which a series of nonconformist ministers philosophically led the revolution. So there was in the United States no impulse to rob religion of its psychological or moral power. To be sure, twentieth-century Prohibition does partake of religious passion, but it was in no way a substitute for it. America has its own passions, but they remain religious, while in Europe religion has been channelled into politics.

The great philosopher of this political religion was Rousseau in his chapter on civil religion in *The Social Contract*. He proposed having a national political religion that would control the state. His criticism of Christianity was that it was otherworldly and made for passive citizens. Nationalism became one of the most significant manifestations of politics, and made a secular substitute for religion. An enemy of religion could be a political replacement for it.

Even though he was a nationalist, Mazzini had a special concern for individualism; the individual functions through the association and the nation to a universal world. Mazzini conceived of a universal cosmos in which each nation has its special purpose. His theory of historical development, moving from the individual to the nation to a universal world, was reminiscent of the historicism of Maistre and Condorcet. The finger of God moved through history by means of the nation which in modern times became the mediator of destiny.

Nationalism bore a special relationship to democracy. The Rousseauian concept meant full participatory democracy, while the traditionalist approach, that of Burke and the conservatives, thought nationalism was exemplified by the status quo. A third perspective was that of the middle-class nationalism of the liberals. But from Rousseau on we inevitably find nationalism; it becomes an emotion that every movement seeks to capitalize on. French conservativism, once France was deeply nationalistic, seized on that emotion. Mid-nineteenth-century liberals did, too. Yet the movement of both conservative and liberal nationalism is not as vibrant a one as that which comes from the totalitarian concept of Rousseau and the Jacobins.

The logic of nationalism implied full democracy in the sense that all men of the community are to be brothers. There is also an inner connection between such a democracy and a nationalism which implies the concept of a universal community. It does not mean that there cannot be nondemocratic nationalism. But the more there is full and equal participation, the more feelings of brotherhood and solidarity can be capitalized on.

Democracy and nationalism in the nineteenth century were interrelated. But there is a force in nationalism that both leads to democracy and tends to destroy it. The supremacy of the nation in the international sphere means that authoritarianism can easily arise. Mazzini himself represents a convergence of democracy and nationalism; but it was the power politics of Camillo Cavour, which overlooked democratic propositions, that finally achieved Italian unity. In Germany liberal nationalism looked beautiful in 1848 but did not produce nationhood; the Bismarckian solution was imposed from above. Nationalism leads in the direction of power and imperialism, and has a tendency toward authoritarianism. Admittedly, great imperial countries have also been democratic: England, France, and even the United States. Nationalism leads first in the direction of democracy, and then away from it.

It was Mazzini's notion that if each nation attained an independent destiny then the world would be in good shape. World peace would be attained by the independence of nations. E. H. Carr in his *The Twenty Years Crisis* pointed out that this notion is a reflection on the international plane of the old proposition on the national level of a natural harmony of interests in which the atomic elements peacefully collide. Mazzini applied to international politics the essential liberal principles. Though he went beyond the simple static liberalism of Bentham, the French liberals, and the philosophes of the eighteenth century, when he came to his final resolution of world peace he relied on the same principles that he had largely overcome because of the socialist influence on him. His faith in an invisible hand that would organize the international universe was an indication of his failure to overcome the omissions of the earlier liberals.

21

Historic Success and Failure

A renewed outburst of liberalism took place in the nineteenth century. How did these liberals handle the question of a free society and the relation of the state to its attainment? They displayed remarkable creativity in the area of the mechanics of the state, yet the basic social evasion of the eighteenth century continued. Their ingenuity about freedom in the context of politics was not extended to the social realm.

The English utilitarians made the basic contribution to the question of the free state. They brought the concept of political freedom to a fulfillment; a choice between alternative sets of government reflects the institutional core of parliamentary government. The basis for this, however, was not quite perfect as long as they relied exclusively on self-interest, which was only a fragmentary psychological insight; as John Stuart Mill pointed out in opposition to his own father's theory, rulers have to be conditioned by more than grim sadism if power is ever to be voluntarily relinquished. Yet Bentham had enunciated the fundamental principle of the alternation of governments.

The French liberals supplemented the raw utilitarian structure. Constant developed the conception of the legislative process to execute the underlying notion of representation. He thought in terms of a Cabinet, a loyal opposition, and competing parties. The principle of dislocability, freedom of choice between rulers, was spelled out in a party system. Self-interest was not enough to support this competition; Constant groped for the insight that underlying this had to be some fundamental moral cohesion of the society. This primary correspondence between social and political systems had to exist for the liberal system to work effectively.

Political and social insights in England contrasted with those in France; the trend in English thought was to emphasize the simple scheme of representation based on the functioning of self-interest, while the French stressed the need for unity. It was a historic paradox, for England in 1832 was emerging from a solid organic community, while France was tormented by conflict between irreconcilable principles. The concept of raw self-interest in England was an attempt to shatter their organic solidarity. Burke was the permanent philosopher of British society, and Bentham's theory was an attempt to counter this. France was in effect a broken society, and its liberal thinkers stressed elements in political philosophy that were concerned with moral cohesion.

Political theory is the dream life of politics. Instead of being a version of what already exists in a society, it can be seen as a reflection of the yearnings, or the absence of prevailing circumstance. French liberal thought was a manifestation of a ruptured society lacking a general will. German society was still seeking to conquer particularism, and therefore the notions of community and the state were part of a yearning for the nonexistent. The American case illustrates why a country can have relatively little political thought at all; the nation was in such full agreement on its fundamental morality that political philosophy did not have to get going in the first place. (The experience of the American Civil War becomes the brief exception that proves the general rule.) Political thought represents the aspirations of a political order and not just its description.

In relating the free state to a free society, the principle of sovereignty in Bentham and Austin contained the mistake of arrogating all legitimate coercion to state power. A propensity of liberal thought in its earlier stages was to see the state as the only legitimate coercive body. Despite what can be said against such an outlook, the state still should have the special responsibility of setting limits to the constraints that can be imposed by corporate bodies over individuals. The coercion of the state differs from the power of any group. Here Constant's notion of individual rights, and John Stuart Mill's concept of liberty, become relevant. Mazzini too thought the state becomes the guardian of individual rights in the social realm.

General Motors has great coercive power; but the solution is not to nationalize that corporation but to erect a Ford plant across the street. This does not mean that the state should not still continue to relate to these corporations; it has the right to inhibit perversions of authority. But the state's coercion is of a special kind—it can not permit slavery and murder, for example.

The state has to be especially concerned with a wide conception of welfare. Mazzini's distinction between national and corporate group interests is relevant. In war, the state can exert power over all groups for the sake of survival. Even after we agree in repudiating the eighteenth century and Bentham, the state should still retain a special role. In the revolt against feudalism the state was seen as the only legitimate source of coercion, which was a big mistake. But it is impossible to deny that the state's coercion is not the same kind as that of General Motors and Ford, although both are highly restrictive.

The drift of mid-nineteenth-century liberalism was to give up the point of its departure about the state; still, many unresolved problems remained. It did make a notable contribution in terms of the forward movement of parliamentary democracy. This was an advance over the eighteenth century, and Bentham stands in some sense for an improvement over Voltaire. Parliamentarism is an achievement as opposed to simple absolute despotism. The great institutional deposit of liberalism in the nineteenth century was the development of parliamentary systems of democracy. Although it was less true in Italy and Germany, the theoretical contribution of liberal thought, if not its historic residue, was parliamentary mechanics and institutions.

The social context of this political advance was another question. Again and again thinkers sensed the presence of great new societal coercions, yet could not work out a liberal solution to this problem. The social world was left pretty much in the same condition as it had been in the eighteenth century. Liberalism failed to extend its political ingenuity to the social realm. After the Reaction's immense affirmation of the significance and complexity of society, how could liberals continue to avoid this very question? That the conservatives pointed out this world of sociology and social coercion raises the question of how liberalism as a movement could be a historic success and a doctrinal failure at the same time. From a loose Hegelian view this would be impossible. Mid-nineteenth-century liberalism would be a synthesis between societal evasion and its affirmation; liberty would by now be defined in social terms.

Yet to the extent that struggles in history are those of interest, what happened becomes understandable. If history is only the fulfillment of ideals, it would be impossible to succeed and be a doctrinal failure. The reactionaries failed even though they had their thoroughly good point. History is not simply the evolution of an ideal; what happens historically is also a struggle of vested forces. The problem of understanding society in terms of freedom, and the creation of an idea of a new social order, was not in the interest of nineteenth-century liberalism to solve.

The advantage of the middle class lay in social evasion. The triumph of the bourgeoisie and its relationship to liberalism does not exhaust that tradition of thought, but the class connection in the nineteenth century is impossible to deny. All of the liberals (except maybe Mazzini) advocated a limitation on suffrage even in the political realm. A revival of Aristotelian middle-class theory can be found in Brougham, Macaulay, and the French liberals. When they are self-consciously bourgeois they think power should be given to the middle class as the best. In a way Marx was merely repeating the argument of the bourgeoisie. They had affirmed that the state should belong to the middle class; he proclaimed that the state did belong to the middle class. Marx reiterated many liberal platitudes, even if his irony was often missed.

How can any movement sustain itself historically despite its doctrinal evasion? So long as the conditions are ripe for historical ascendancy, the limits that interests place upon thought are no barrier for success. Historical conditions can compensate for doctrinal failure. The strength and the universality of a theory must be great enough to offset its evasions. The immense appeal of the free state was so great that it more than balanced liberalism's social evasion. The ideal of parliamentary advance captured the imagination of many groups.

In 1830, 1832, and 1848 the masses followed the middle class in an attempt to democratize the political system. The new groups being turned up were enchanted by the political objectives of the middle class. Liberalism did not answer the Reaction because it did not need to respond to it.

The political thought of any epoch never exceeds what circumstances require of it; all arguments are linked to the existence of social forces. Conservatism suffered from the flaw that its concept of society was harnessed to the feudal order which had no chance to survive; the Reaction posed therefore no vital challenge to the middle class. Political thought never goes beyond the needs of necessity. It is always important to watch the arguments thinkers can avoid answering. The points that can be evaded, not the ones that can be handled successfully, constitute what is historically significant.

Marxism today has had its argument destroyed, yet it keeps going. It does not need to answer the most devastating criticisms that have been advanced. It has succeeded in spite of the annihilation of its political thought. Similarly liberalism in relation to the Reaction ignored the exposé of its evasions. A movement is not tested by points it can answer but measured by its capacity to go forward in spite of those arguments. The refutation of a movement that continues to be successful is an indication that it has a vital grip on thought. The affirmative force is now Marxism, as it was liberalism in the nineteenth century. We are today subject to a species of slavery to the categories of Marx.

If our central problem, the concept of a free society, can be evaded, why worry about it? A movement can be successful without paying attention to this central question. If the problem could be permanently avoided it would be devastating. But the evasive technique did not persist; at some point the question of free society would become the problem of the age. Liberal evasion was running out of time; by 1848 a new movement challenged liberalism on the ground of social freedom.

In Part IV I will examine the point at which our logical preoccupation becomes the key to historic success or failure, and thus the problem of the age. Our issue becomes historically real. The name socialism is itself interesting, since it highlights that it proposes to deal with the problem of society. It appeared first in an Owenite magazine, and meant then collective in contrast to individual action.

The fundamental insight of the Reaction fulfills itself in socialism. It took the social insight that the conservatives could not impose on history first and succeeded by means of it. The antecedent figure to Marx is Burke. The deepest doctrinal connection exists between the sociology of conservatism and that of socialism. Yet the problem of society was not developed by a vital social force until the rise of socialism.

The social insight which had been clothed in medieval-sounding arguments now reappears successfully in a new guise; socialism represents a repetition of a key point of the Reaction. With Marx, though, the societal aspect is now permeated with liberalism; he refurbished the social insight of the conservatives with egalitarian and libertarian doctrines. Disraeli, Carlyle, and the feudal socialists could not succeed because the proletariat would not accept the old corporate solution, but they will adopt the same essential idea if developed in terms of liberalism.

Marx and Engels made the greatest strategic contribution. The new proletariat emerges out of a liberal society that has left feudalism far behind. This class was born in liberal society, its instinctive language was that of liberalism. The falsity of liberal atomism meant the emergence of a proletariat bitter about its social oppression.

It was not individualism but collectivism that called forth this new class. Industrialism socialized labor; liberal society collectivized the working class. Out of the gap between theory and practice in the new world of liberalism the socialist movement was created. Collectivism was a product of capitalism; the proletariat could only approach its struggle with a liberal vocabulary. A product of liberal society must speak in its language. In the gulf between individualist doctrine and collectivist society, the concept of individual liberty would be extended to the new society that had been created. Given this situation social insight was bound to take form in a liberal framework.

Socialism was the first concrete effort to deal with the problem we have been addressing; it harnessed the Enlightenment ideal of liberty to the social world. Socialism becomes the historical fulfillment of our concerns; it was structured in the situation that the fulfillment of the issue was in the hands of the proletariat. But did this new class solve the problem, and did socialism offer the right answer?

Part IV

SOCIALISM

22

Robert Owen

In England, where the industrial revolution was furthest advanced, Owen's basic psychological assumptions were Benthamite; this was true even though Marx called him a "utopian socialist." Owen did proceed from the hedonistic criterion of the greatest happiness. Yet the difference between Owen and Bentham was considerable. In Owen's view Bentham's formula can never work because happiness is not a function of individual self-interest but the result of a collective feeling of altruism. Owen wanted to eliminate private self-interest. The substitution of altruism for self-interest had to lead the utilitarian system to catastrophe, since for Bentham individual self-interest was the ultimate drive of man.

Owen denies this part of Benthamite psychology; according to him human nature is instead determined by the environment. He thought selfishness can be made to yield to altruism through a basic change in the environment. In Owen's view Bentham mistook a transient and relative motive for the permanent culture. Locke and liberal environmentalism was an obvious part of Owen's heritage. Yet the physiocrats wanted to manipulate the environment in order to free the individual, and the utilitarians relied on legislation to get people to operate in socially constructive channels; both schools of thought assumed an atomistic psychology, whereas Owen wanted to eliminate egoism.

If, as Owen thought, men are completely the determined product of their environment, how can they ever transform it? Radical social determinism leaves little ground for change. The problem can also be found in current anthropolitical doctrine. Fromm, for example, proposes the concept of a historical personality; he talks in terms of medieval rather than Renaissance man. But if personality is nothing but the reflection of the outside world, how do things change? Men would seem to be shaped without being able to do anything about it. Yet radicalism implies that something must have escaped the impact of the environment.

Owen did propose that people are subject to the processes of persuasion. But receptivity to argument is dominated by the environment that you are seeking to destroy. This is the sort of circularity Owen gets into when he tries to rob man of all freedom. Cultural determinism is often associated with modern social science. But any consistent drive for change shows there is something apart from the determined elements in man, and therefore Owen himself implicitly contradicts determinism.

In fact the influence of society is plural rather than monolithic; any cultural determinism forces the individual to face the problem of choice and action in relation to the social order. Two ways out of naive cultural determinism can be seen; first, some quality of freedom escapes from its shaping impact, and that is why we get individual freedom in a moral or psychological sense. Secondly, no cultural impact is monolithic but rather a series of such influences.

Owen does not adopt our solution; for him the monolithic impact of a culture of self-interest creates self-interested man. Marx too thought that capitalistic culture produces capitalistic man. But one cannot explain change in Owen's terms. He does emphasize hereditary and constitutional factors in personality, thus he is not an utter social determinist. Yet he still is not saved from the implications of his approach, for he does not investigate the interaction of hereditary and cultural factors. If Owen explored this interplay, he would have had some kind of Freudian "id" factor resisting the force of culture. He would have raised a point against environmentalism. But his objective was to establish the possibility of altruism and social longing by taking a different tack; otherwise he would have been impelled to see that the interaction of hereditary and environment would have to produce an infinite variety of individuals. He wanted a society of cooperation and solidarism, and the discovery of diversity and multiplicity would have ruined his system.

Owen's criticism of egotism was an aspect of his approach to communal personality. He wanted completely to eliminate present society, the whole culture producing the existing egotistic man; he proposed to do away with the coercions of property, family, education, and religion in order to produce a perfectly harmonious world with an equitable distribution of the wealth produced by the industrial revolution. Once culture is changed, egotists are made into altruists and the full fruit of industrialism will be achieved. Owen thought machine power a blessing and had great faith in industrialization.

Owen's blasts at individualism were not really a criticism of too much freedom, but an attack on the oppression which this principle had given rise to socially. He wanted to exchange one form of society for another; he was not trying to substitute collectivism for individualism, but saying that the concept of individualism produces disorganized society and he wanted to achieve an organized one. What Owen attacks is the society of the liberal movement, not any artificial individualism which it is conceded does not exist.

As far as the growth of democracy and the creation of parliamentary institutions, Owen did not think anything of it; he had disregard and contempt for the political achievements of mid-nineteenth-century liberalism. For him the great preoccupation of liberalism over different forms of government, as with the French liberals, was false, and he was not concerned with the expansion of the suffrage. To Owen none of the liberals had solved the problem of the social order and its life, and the only way to measure achievement is by the standard of a solution to the social question. For Owen all governments are founded on a corrupt basis.

This dismissal is not a valid one. The very solution of the social issue of freedom was bound up with the liberal accomplishment. The problem of achieving Enlightenment ideals has to be solved in the state first. The working classes of England gained much from the extension of the suffrage; politics impinged on the social realm. Owen's indictment was false because the one failure did not cancel out the other. His kind of preoccupation with the social question meant the dismissal by the socialist movement of the positive achievements of liberals in the realm of politics, and a movement emerged which was to discredit the solid advances of the liberals. Owen thought that forms of a state are inconsequential, and that all of them have been founded on a bad society. Even liberalism's successes are liable to go down the drain because of its failures. A partial lapse is a threat to everything.

According to idealist thinking the good cannot get lost with the bad; but we find a solid point being shoved away because of an inadequate one. It was an inverted form of the problem of the conservatives—their insights into society were lost because they were trapped in obsolete forms. It was ironic that socialism might pass up the political achievements of liberalism because of the evasion of the social point that conservatives made. Liberalism did not reply to the social insights of the Reaction, and socialism passed up the political insights of liberalism because of the evasion of the social question. Mixtures of truth and error are passing each other by in history; the historical process does not produce a wholeness. Something not too rational has been taking place.

For Owen the problem of politics did not disappear; rather, the social issue absorbed the political question. He proposed to organize society into communities made up of great families, organizations that would embrace man in all his activities. His institutional scheme had eight classes organized according to age rather than existing classifications of wealth. Each class would have a function; the last class would govern the community with the oldest people conducting foreign relations and travel. He was tireless in his details. He suggested a Rousseauian solution: to identify society with politics creates a solidaristic result. Government was to have the final power in all matters under its control, but essentially it was a proposal to nationalize coercions. Owen had in mind a network of small polises all over the world, a kind of pluralistic totalitarianism.

But what about freedom? How free did Owen leave us? Bentham had approached the question of freedom in terms of how to keep governors from ruling badly. For Owen this problem did not appear since human nature will have been changed;

governors, being elderly people, will be superlatively altruistic. One can grant that they will be altruists, yet still they may still differ; conflict can arise as a result of imperfect agreement among altruists. Men can still disagree concerning the common good, and conflicts of judgment can exist. But Owen thought this would be impossible; societal good is unitary, and everyone will be shaped by the same environment and therefore will agree. Owen was avoiding individual uniqueness; identical human creatures were to be produced by a common environment. Everyone was the product of one culture; in a parallel way Locke thought that since all men see the law of nature, they arrive at the same conclusions.

Owen knew that technical problems arise as you move from the concept of egotism to that of altruism. But he dismissed these as mere transitional ones to be ironed out by consulting a third party. Government was purely an administrative matter. Yet politics has to do with reconciliation of conflict; once it is eliminated, government is reduced to mere problems of administration. The issue of street lighting, for example, should not pose political questions. For Owen spontaneous unanimity will arise, and there will never be a conflict between the rational and particular will. The premise that the rational will functions in all cases eliminates the question of politics, which was the tendency in all socialist thought. Political problems are done away with by the emphasis on changing the environment. Owen is not really talking about government in the normal sense of the coercions on men in any given context. The institutions of government are transformed into those of administration, as of a factory; he appears to have had in mind the administration of things rather than of men.

His socialism had implications for the liberty of the solitary individual. He thought there can be no propagation of old errors that would infect the young people. Government was to change the whole environment, and therefore the idea of a free press would be ridiculous. Also, he does not worry about the problem that might arise if an individual wanted to leave one Owenite community and go to another. But after all, the movement between associations is the critical point at which liberty appears. This issue was scarcely touched on by Owen. Any competition of associations, related to choice, would horrify him for it would introduce "pandemonium." He thought human beings will not experience dissatisfaction or frustration in their new environment. No one would want to change; rather, he assumed that the individual will be happy in harmony with the group.

Unique factors of individuality can be expected to produce restlessness and the desire for change. An individual constitutionally may be led to move. But the problem of individual liberty does not appear in Owen. Just as politics has evaporated so has the issue of individual liberty; neither conflict nor frustration is admitted.

Owen gives up the problem of politics by fusing it with society, reasoning the problem of freedom out of existence. Political questions are annihilated in a strange vengeance of intellectual history. A movement that came to deal with the social question was so concerned with it that it destroyed the achievements of liberalism. Owen eliminates politics by a series of social definitions. Socialism's approach was not to answer the political problem but rather to do away with it conceptually.

In Owen there is no solution to our problem of the free society and the relation of the state to its attainment. He destroys what political advances were made, absorbing politics into the social sphere. His work eliminates the normative problem we have been dealing with. It may be true that most societies handle freedom by trying to shape the individual so that he is unconscious of all the coercions that impinge on him. But societies are never completely successful in this effort; there are always some areas of conscious tension, and it is at these points that the struggle for freedom focuses. Otherwise the history of society would be stationary.

Given our historical analysis, it would be impossible that Owen be all that the socialist movement could produce. The working classes were infected with the liberal idea, and Owen's ideals were not framed in its terms. His one-class system was not designed to solve the individualistic aspirations of the proletariat. Neither Comte nor Carlyle could gain a grip on the emergent proletariat either. Owen overlooks the fact that the liberal ideas of equality and self-government are inevitable.

The industrial revolution had failed to supply enough in the way of concrete freedom, although it provided plenty of meaningless liberal autonomy. Owen dissociated the problem of poverty from freedom, which represented an evasion of a modern reality.

Owen was primarily concerned with the elimination of "pandemonium," replacing it with rationality. His genteel spirit was like that of an efficiency expert; he wanted peace. He did not like social noise, confusion, or chaos. Yet this approach had little to do with the dynamic appeal of socialism; the elimination of conflict was not the concern of the working class. The problems of the industrial revolution were intensely societal, including the loss of status for some workers. Conflicts existed both between and within groups; poverty and misery existed for the mass of industrial workers, while Owen sought to eliminate conflict and thereby solve all the problems of society.

Marxists would call Owen a "class collaborationist." He wanted to bring the bourgeoisie and the proletariat together quietly. Owen's socialist thought contained elements of continuity with nineteenth-century liberalism, although he wanted to eliminate its achievements in connection with the problem of politics itself. Still, it contained things that were bound to be discarded. Owen was indifferent to the ideals of liberty, equality, and fraternity, and excessively concerned with peace and rationality. Marx will represent the completion of some of these socialist tendencies, yet later there will be a reversal in a more rationalistic direction in the thought of the British Fabians. Nonetheless the two achievements of liberalism and socialism do not come together, and history does not amount to a Hegelian cumulative unfolding.

23

François Fourier

Socialism had a central preoccupation with the social dimension of existence; Owen was a radical environmentalist, for although he recognized independent elements in human nature like heredity, still he emphasized the impact of the outside world in shaping personality. Superficially Fourier is often called a nonenvironmentalist. He stressed the fixed character of human nature. He had a theory of essential human passions, giving no indication that they ever changed over time. The concept of immutable human nature is not the usual tool of a radical reformer, since it seems to pose barriers to social change; the Reaction had stressed a fixed quality of human evil requiring external coercion.

Yet in Fourier this approach becomes the underpinning to a system of radical change. Passions exist but they are intrinsically good; they have been perverted and frustrated by social coercions. Once society is reconstructed so that it releases these drives, all life will be different and harmony will be instituted; a type of perennial humanist demand, reminiscent of Rousseau in *Emile,* recurs. Human nature is fixed, yet society is threatened because it has gotten out of gear with these passions. Fourier had no vision of evil in his conception of human nature, and therefore unlike Burke and Bonald he thought social coercions were unnecessary.

For Fourier, as for Owen, the key to social change was environmental. He did not propose to transform basic human nature, but what amounts to the same thing—the behavior of man. Fourier, with his proposal to liberate human nature, had the same reformist message as Owen. Concepts of a static and plastic human nature can both involve radical alterations in society to produce a change in conduct. The strands of environmentalism and humanism can lead to the same result even if they proceed from different premises. Fourier postulated a good human core in human nature that only required liberation.

Social institutions distort passions, which is why society has splintered into competitive institutions. It is reminiscent of Owen's dislike of pandemonium. Fourier's specific opposition to competition, conflict, and duplication raises questions, for he was one of those socialists opposed to industrial society because of its incoherence and disorganization. He proposed to construct a new society in accord with human nature to achieve harmony. There were in his view twelves passsions, and three classses of them—*material, social,* and *serial.* The system was patently absurd as psychology, but the idea of serial passions was designed to account for restlessness, the urge for variety and change. Once society is correctly based on these drives Fourier thought that they all would work spontaneously together. In modern society the serial passions, which are really amiable, produce war; in a reconstructed social order the same drives lead to progress. In his quest for unity and solidarity Fourier suggested that the serial passions have a harmonious destiny.

Now liberal society was marked by brute group conflict. This social stress was the pandemonium that Owen complained about. Yet it also produced greater unity of production and less duplication. The drive of the industrial revolution led to two impulses: first of all a jungle of class conflict, group and individual competition, and then second a division of labor, with economy and a rationalizing of the system. The main thrust of utopian socialism was engendered by the industrial revolution and an extension of its ethos; it desired to eliminate the chaos produced by capitalism. The principle of division of labor had not succeeded enough; centralization and unification of production were needed.

Fourier had a passion for economy; he thought great savings could be achieved by socialist remedies. In objecting to the

existence of too many kitchens he was raising a capitalist principle against capitalism. His economizing temperament was trying to fulfill a rationalizing impulse of capitalism. A drive for
making effort efficient was being utilized to assail the capitalist
system itself.

The physiocrats, Adam Smith, and the Benthamites were all
interested in a basic transformation in the ideals of the feudal
system. In inquiring into the source of value, the liberal movement, by unloosing the norm of economy against capitalism,
sent forth a potential weapon against itself. For the socialists
stressed productiveness and abundance. Liberalism also had
released an ideal of liberty that got turned against itself by
socialism.

The concept of class was also a basic one which the liberal
movement had used against feudalism, and the proletariat took
over this notion too. And the theory of surplus value was
utilized first by the physiocrats and then by Marx. The whole
basic apparatus of socialist thought was produced by liberal
thinkers. Liberalism is the ultimate author of all reform
thought, and the bourgeoisie the only imaginative force in
modern political theory.

Fourier emphasized the waste and social wickedness of conflict. We are reminded of the Reaction's concern with societal
cohesion and unity. The link between Fourier and the French
conservatives had been seen by Michels. For the reactionaries,
conflict stems from bad passions; external force is needed to
eliminate it. Fourier and Owen thought that the trouble stems
from the evils of the social system. This principal of externality
dissolves the matter: merely change the society and men will
spontaneously unite in a harmony of interests. Unlike the
Reaction, conflict was not natural for Fourier. Socialism offers
reminders of both liberal and reactionary values.

In the aspirations of the new social groups the first idea of
economic unity was an appealing one. The prospect of abundance and the creation of more goods was tremendous. Yet
tension remained. Neither Fourier nor Owen associated themselves with the aspirations of the proletariat for freedom and
equality in the Enlightenment's sense. Class conflict meant
breathing the iconoclastic and revolutionary spirit; Marxism

transferred to socialist thought the liberal mentality of 1789. But Fourier was a "collaborationist" waiting for a wealthy patron to appear at a specified hour in the early afternoon every day; he had no sense of the revolutionary quality of the proletarian experience.

Socialism was the reflection in proletarian terms of the bourgeois experience. And therefore any failure to transform the meaning of revolution into proletarian categories was bound to backfire. In the underlying yearning to duplicate the middle class's experience, the French Revolution cannot be left out. The wealthy man will not come to agree with Fourier because it is against his interest to do so. It is a neglected point that the proletariat wanted the revolutionary experience; this did not necessarily mean the use of force but it did imply a clash with employers.

Fourier was out of gear on this point. For him the nature of the socialist community was a set of little associations. They were not especially socialistic but more like joint stock companies. An individual bought money and goods, invested and got shares with dividends. In the distribution of profits Fourier assigned a significant share to capital as well as to labor and talent; he did not rule out the profit motive. Fourier's associations were very close to business corporations. Any idea of class position in relation to capitalism was not there; his outlook was removed from the concept that profit motive is a source of conflict.

Fourier looked at reform from the standpoint of the individual. Titles were to be handed out to satisfy serial passions, even though titles carried no political power. Unlike Owen, Fourier proposed that the government of the phalanxes be elected. Owen thought that task of government could be determined by age; Claude Saint-Simon, in Comte's tradition, relied on experts. But Fourier had a Benthamite impulse and wanted an elected government.

Fourier considered individual freedom a significant factor. Owen did not discuss whether pluralism of associations had to be related to the individual's possible movement. But Fourier directly confronted this issue and said that the urge for variety, ambition, and the passion for change creates the problem of individuality. Fourier's answer was that the individual can choose any society he pleases at any time. This individual choice was buttressed by the principle of property; one could invest in another community. He appreciated the individual's place in a system of multiplicity supported by the right of profit. He relied on the market mechanism to preserve individuality. He recognized the value of difference in wealth and reward, and made no attempt at establishing uniformity. The individual's shares are mobile and can be sold for the sake of moving; one is free to leave. Here we can find the influence of associationalism on Mazzini, and his concern for the nature of group life. Mazzini links Fourier to the liberal movement; but for Fourier no nationalism existed, only the unity of the world.

How good was his solution? The opportunity of choice is more brutally limited in the social world than Fourier believed. He thought people could move anywhere. But that expression of individual choice is often restricted by coercions that cannot be overcome. A constant free choice of jobs is at odds with the requirements of industrial society in disciplining people. The problem of choice is surrounded by a highly coercive context.

Fourier's utopian concept of society makes possible his extreme answer. He laid down a principle of universal attraction and unity so that by definition no conflict will exist between the individual and the group. Harmony meant that the passion for unity would never counteract the drive for variety. It was another version of Smith's invisible hand. In the implicit union of Fourier's passional scheme there will never be a contradiction between two urges. Fourier thought that if society were properly constructed spontaneous harmony would appear.

Yet he evaded the real problem of liberty in society. His government would have no use if such universal harmoniousness existed. He was talking about the administration of things and not politics. The issue of conflict between individuality and the needs of society would be dissolved simply because of his conviction about the nature of the passional system. One does not really need government in Fourier's view because it arises from disharmony, that is, when points of view cannot be reconciled smoothly.

We have here the death of political thought and politics. In Fourier's scheme politics and society blend; the phalanstery embraces everything. He can not be considered totalitarian because he did not acknowledge that any problem of coercion can appear. The theory of Fourier ends with Owen; the problem of freedom was solved by psychological definition, the issue of politics eliminated, and government reduced to administration. He proposed a synthesis of government and society.

Fourier, like Owen, blasts the political preoccupations of liberals. Owen thought that controversies over forms of government were unimportant. Fourier considered that all efforts at revolution with political objectives were of no significance. The elimination of political problems in this social analysis leads to a dismissal of politics as trivial.

In this way a constructive advance was cancelled out by the socialist movement since they were preoccupied with an evaded problem to the exclusion of legitimate liberal contributions. Political revolutions cannot be said to have accomplished nothing. The parliamentary state was produced thanks to 1832 and 1867, 1830 and 1848. In these birthpangs of parliamentarism the political structure of democracy was erected. Socialism denies the significance of this achievement because of the problem of the liberal evasion of society. A relevant failure can destroy a significant accomplishment.

The Reaction got its revenge for having been passed up when socialism ignored the liberals. Half-truths were cancelling each other out, and arguments were being eliminated by being avoided. Would the socialists succeed in shattering the distinction between the state and society? Could the political achievements of liberalism be preserved and the social problem still be solved? Marxian criticism emerges out of these issues.

24

Karl Marx

Proudhon was not a utopian socialist in the sense of Fourier and Owen; he was an individualist, a philosopher of the independent peasantry, and as such he was concerned with the question of the relation of the individual to the association. Fourier, in talking about the movement between phalanxes, stressed too heavily the possibility of universal contractualism. In making an effort to eliminate all coercions, he proposed a pervasive Lockianism of contract. This contractualism dissolving all coercions was even more utopian than the rest of this branch of socialism since it does not recognize the inevitable area of coercion surrounding choice.

The ultimate moralism of Proudhon links him to Rousseau. As a utopian socialist he sought to establish a conflict between the particular and the rational will, and to eliminate tensions due to the lack of fit between the environment and individual. A permanent struggle between an individual's higher and lower self means the presence of the eternal problem of politics; in this way it was restored to the tradition of socialism. By stressing this inevitable inner conflict, Proudhon became an atypical, complicated, and unique figure in this school; his influence was mainly connected with the Owen-Fourier strand of thought with its scheme of associations and criticisms of capitalism.

Marxism had its link to the Hegelian tradition at the same time that it grew out of the earlier ideas of Owen, Fourier, and Proudhon. Owen and Fourier had assailed capitalist liberalism by extending the ethos of economy and rationality that it had generated. The attack on pandemonium was a product of the capitalist principle. A distinct fulfillment of this tendency came in the economic ethos being used so severely against capitalism itself. The theory of value was a physiocratic concern, and its discussion of surplus reflected a search for an economic parasite. Marxism is also a turning of the spirit of capitalism against capitalism; the relation of Marx and the physiocrats is very strong. Between Quesnay and Marx we have come full circle with the original liberal principle being directed against itself.

The labor theory of value and the concept of surplus value are key Marxian contributions and account for a fresh perception of social coercions. Labor is held to be the source of value; raw materials come to a factory where they get transformed in price. Marx estimates value in terms of the market economy. He thinks that labor produces the central difference: the value of a commodity is determined by the quantity of labor necessary for its production. He avoids the obvious criticisms, such as the more labor the greater the worth; value is determined by labor which is socially necessary, within a general degree of competition and an average amount of skill and technology. A more basic point is raised by the issue of whether it is human labor alone that creates the price differential. Machinery plays a role whose contribution Marx does not deny, but he thought machinery or constant capital derives its value from labor. Marx looks on it as merely stored-up labor.

A fundamental issue is the surplus theory of value which has links to the physiocrats and the idea of parasites. According to Marx's subsistence theory of wages, under capitalism labor is viewed as a commodity; the worth of its market contribution to production is less than labor's true value. Surplus labor is the basis of surplus value. Subsistence is what workers get paid, and wages are always lower than labor's contribution to value.

A concept of economic parasitism is being used against the class that invented the idea of surplus in the first place. The basic ideas of liberalism are being turned against itself by the socialist movement. The adaptation of capitalism to socialist philosophy is relatively minor. Given the coercions of the new society and the ideals of 1789, there was an inevitable drive for the Enlightenment norms to get turned against liberal society. Those elements of liberty and equality were being applied to liberal society's own neglected coercions. Marx is not like Carlyle, Disraeli, or Comte, who tried to create a new feudal relation. His concept of surplus value implies a principle of perpetual conflict of interests; another's good contradicts our good. Fourier proposed to wait for wealthy persons, and Owen was a capitalist himself; both had a solution to coercions by "collaborating" with the capitalists themselves. Marx is saying that conflict is so basic that you can never expect capitalists to be reasoned into a solution or even a compromise. Marxism is the final dissolution of the idea of a harmony of interests.

Is this analysis of living labor as the source of value valid? For Marx profits cannot come from a machine, even though it contributes value. Machinery imparts worth but not greater than the value of stored-up labor; it depreciates in proportion as it contributes. We can get no more out of a machine than we have put into it, as opposed to its amounting to a net productivity. The physiocrats had idealized the role of land; but it is the peculiar quality of living labor alone, according to Marx, to produce more than it costs.

If profits come only from living labor, why should capitalists ever introduce machinery? One might then maximize profits by maximizing living labor, and therefore stick to the handicraft world. If fixed capital were no source of profit, the least profitable entrepreneur should have the least labor and the most machinery. Among different industries, the more use of labor the higher the level of profits should be; for example, agriculture should be more profitable than the steel industry.

In the third volume of *Capital* Marx tries to solve this problem. He averages profits in an unsuccessful effort to establish his position; the actual empirical result does not confirm the Marxian proposition. It is necessary to assume that increasing value is derived from living labor *and* from capital itself. Capital is past labor; but profit is created by a partnership of the labor of the living with the labor of the dead. Everyone contributing to the surplus should be rewarded. All people should benefit who keep the social system going which permits us to have the economic technique. Conservative theory argues that the transmission of technique is the product of a whole social system; therefore they would allocate rewards far more broadly than Marx would. Certain aspects of society are more relevant to such transmission; a professor of physics is by this standard more significant than an heiress like Doris Duke. One could retain the criteria for allocation in terms of utility, yet embrace more people than the laborers in a factory.

Eventually under capitalism there was an increasing separation of ownership from management. Marx had envisaged a capitalist who worked in the plant, an actual entrepreneur. Now one can own stocks and bonds, engaging in ownership but without working. We do in fact tax so-called unearned income more heavily.

Apart from the issue of social equality, Marxism is relevant in the area of freedom. He had a valid insight relating to the worker and his labor time; in selling labor, the individual also sells himself. Furthermore, much despotism is possible in the factory setting. In being subordinate to factory rule a new hierarchy of workers develops; skill had been relatively equal in a handicraft society. In addition to the selling of the self there is the introduction of a vast inequality in status to fit the needs of machinery, which require small pools of trained technicians. A former equity of skill was eliminated by machines; while an increase in skills takes place for a few, the many are reduced to highly unskilled positions. According to the theory of surplus value, profit comes mainly from unskilled labor. This involves not merely a loss of talent to society, but the beginning of the frustration of capacities that go unfulfilled under capitalism.

Factory life has its frustrations, such as monotony. The sense of control coming from the production of a total commodity is gone; the psychological satisfaction is missing. Industrialization produced the alienation of the individual worker from the totality of the industrial process and the ultimate product itself. Volume I of *Capital* criticizes the compulsions of life in capitalist industrial society; there is a very fine dissection there of the sociology of the factory system. Marx goes further in analysis than Owen, Fourier, or Proudhon. He makes a powerful indictment in libertarian terms against industrialism.

As for Marx's solutions, he did not deal with them since he

basically was a critic; his was a philosophy of capitalism rather than socialism. Other socialists had rejected the traditional concept of a unified state, and it played no role in the achievement of their objectives. Marx did argue that the state was the instrument of the ruling class, and it partly exercised its power by imposing its values on its age. But Marx drew the conclusion that the working class must have a state of its own. He was not advocating parliamentarianism but the unitary state, as did Bentham and the liberals. Here he conflicted with earlier socialists, and in this connection Mikhail Bakunin fought him within the First International.

Ultimately Marx envisaged a stateless society in which human nature would be changed; as such he was duplicating Owen and Fourier, in that the problem of freedom would be solved once more by definition. Class warfare is accompanied by the power of the state; with the abolition of classes, the state of necessity must wither away. The liberal vision of automatic harmony resurfaces in the Marxian ideal for the future. The ultimate society is both inevitable and cosmopolitan, since like the traditional liberals Marx could not acknowledge the legitimate role of nationalism as a force.

For now, however, Marx made the basic recommendation that the workers seek to expropriate the expropriators. Confronted with fundamental areas of coercion, Marx's remedy is to socialize it or nationalize it. This was essentially an extension of Rousseau's formula; it represents one possible solution of liberty in an actual society. The liberal proposition that all legitimate coercion must come from the state was a product of the drive against feudal society. Rousseau had discovered coercion and nationalized it in the name of liberal principle. Marxism was an extension of this mechanism; the liberal world was held to be untrue, since it contained frightful coercion. The answer is to socialize the area of coercion, and thereby legitimize and dissolve the social chains. Rousseau and Marx share the same relation to liberalism; the proletariat comes across identified with industrial coercion, and in order to create one class Marx suggests first the abolition of classes.

In the relation of liberals of the eighteenth and nineteenth centuries, absolute sovereignty had given way to the parliamentary system. They have the idea of choice, although they do not really implement it. Nineteenth-century liberalism advanced the concept of free contract, but the environment of coercions hems it in.

There is something valid in Marx's solution; an enhancement of freedom does come about with socialization; by participation one can control coercion to a certain extent. One can cast a kind of vote as a proletarian, in that through participation one can influence the nature of factory life. Fabianism later advocated workers' control over industry.

But when the society becomes the sole owner of the instruments of production, the principle of alternatives is shattered; one master and one employer are left. An individual can never find another employer. This is the end of alternatives by means of socialization, a point which Friedrich Hayek makes. If one has both private and state enterprise, one should be grateful for the degree of the former, because there is pluralism in private action. To the extent that nationalization becomes legitimate, the worker votes merely once in awhile, and this ballot is far removed from his position as a worker in a steel mill, for example.

A response to this point comes in syndicalism. There have been attempts to make real the Benthamite principle of dislocability in an industrial context. Yet these devices conflict with the institutional requirements of our society. Pluralism can be in conflict with the national planning of production.

The Marxian indictment goes beyond possible forms of economic production, finding roots in the nature of production itself. These are aspects of industrial life that the Rousseauian principle of socialization does not touch. Some coercions stem not from private property but from the characteristics of industrial society which Marx perceived. Marx's curative response for these criticisms is not coextensive with the diagnosis. He seizes on Rousseau's solution yet the coercions cannot be altered by different papers of ownership. Socialization is not a solution to liberty; it leads ultimately to totalitarianism. Many things are left out in Marx's theories. Yet he succeeded in making the issue of liberty in society the problem of the age, even though he did not solve it himself. He had great insight into coercion, yet socialization as a remedy did not basically touch it. It may be unfair to say that he did not resolve the problem, for the political side of Marxism was an attempt to confront the issue of freedom in a real society of coercion.

Conclusion

Marx's analysis of industrial society was far better than that of the earlier socialist literature. Even compared with the Reaction he was exquisitely preoccupied with social coercions. The conservatives had emphasized inequality, hierarchy, and areas of pressure on the individual in society. But they developed these insights within the framework of the old decadent feudal mythology. Disraeli and Carlyle sought to absorb social substance into the feudal framework. Marx saw factory tyranny, and instead assimilated it into the norms of the Enlightenment. He thought inequality was not inevitable but must be eliminated. Surplus value and the existence of laborers and exploiters were to be abolished. He pointed out hierarchy in order to eliminate it.

The connection of reward with a contribution to constructive activity is an ethical correlary of his surplus value theory. The division between ownership and work first had been made by the physiocrats. Nationalization implies that a degree of freedom is attainable through democratic action. By the manipulation of alternatives, internal democracy can be brought to the economic sphere. The invasion of industrialism so enhanced liberty in this sense as to make for a general increase in the freedom of alternatives.

The danger of Marxism lies in an essentially Rousseauian outcome. Rousseau nationalized coercions, eliminated alternatives, and the state became the only employer. It is a delicate question whether the freedom that was introduced could be offset by the threat; too heavy a burden was placed on the political sphere.

Marxism clashes with the pluralist philosophy we have been developing.

A subtle balance exists between the role of the state in enhancing freedom and limiting it. The internal pluralism within the state ought to be explored. There is a brute limit to what the state can do, which argues for decentralization. Party government does not make a reality of freedom when the state is the only employer. The ideal would be an active state, intensely flexible within, operating inside a plural society.

Marx did not solve the problem of social liberty, nor did anyone else in the nineteenth century. The Marxian cure was not as good as its diagnosis of industrial society. An alteration in the structure of ownership does not touch the basic industrial problem. Marx did aim to reduce the demands on workers; he had in mind the progressive conquest of nature itself—the leap from the physical and material servitude to a condition where the individual is released from material necessity and leisure is enhanced. He wanted to minimize the impact on each individual of the demands of industrial discipline.

Leisure itself raises a new range of problems. One does not attain social liberty by grasping it once and for all. We will confront social coercion elsewhere even after successful leaps of technology. It is an unending nature and process which characterizes the problem of social alternatives.

Marx shared the tendency to dismiss the contributions of nineteenth-century liberalism after he had seized on the significance of the social problem. He applied the economic ethos of capitalism against capitalism. The liberal state is repudiated because of its failure to solve the social problem. Marx was the first to link the Enlightenment ideals to reactionary insights. Socialism first suggests that we can use the state, and then says that the democratic state is an impossible instrument. Since the state is a class tool it cannot fulfill its function as a neutral arbitrator. Class analysis makes possible a more drastic indictment of the parliamentary state; Marx had in mind the state of nineteenth-century liberalism, the regime of Louis Philippe which was in the control of a self-conscious class as advocated by Guizot and Macaulay.

Yet social evils can in fact be ameliorated through parliamentarism by such devices as factory legislation. Marx thought such reforms are characterized by the principle of concessions, they did not go to the foundations of capitalist power. To him they were marginal and soporific for the middle class maintaining its power; the whole democratic state was a facade of capitalist dictatorship.

For Marx the competition of elites and Bentham's kind of alternatives are not real; both choices would be reflections of the ruling bourgeoisie. Marx thought he had located a monopoly. There is much to be said for this theory; economic power does function within what is only a presumably free set of alternatives. But Marx does not succeed in invalidating the parliamentary system either theoretically or institutionally. The experience of the New Deal in America and twentieth-century British socialism show that the democratic system had a viability transcending class power. Marx might see these reform movements as simply middle-class concessions, but that principle of his had altogether too much flexibility to it, so as to be incapable of ever being falsified.

Marx had thought that the social question could not be dealt with without destroying the liberal state. A split in the socialist movement took place, so that figures like Eduard Bernstein, Karl Kautsky, Jean Jaurès, and the Fabians stood against the Leninist trend. Hard-nosed Marxists thought that once parliamentarianism tried social reform, there would be a capitalist reaction, and that this explained the appearance of fascism. Yet fascism arose where Benthamite institutions had never been established. In both Italy and Germany the 1848 revolution had failed. Fascism should instead be related to the historic solution of Bismarck. As a constructive matter the Marxists were wrong; the parliamentary mechanism turns out to have surprising viability.

The democratic state and plural society bear a feasible relation to each other. They permit a maximum of movement within the joints of society. Western democracies have a descriptive reality in terms of the number of alternatives and the freedom of movement available for individuals.

Yet Marxism could do to liberalism what liberalism did to the Reaction. Liberalism's complaints about the lack of democracy were replaced by the Marxist reproach of an absence of adequate socialism. We find the mechanism of half-truths canceling each other out, which becomes a relevant problem for the twentieth century. As one issue blots out another because of the evasion of still a third issue, we confront a senseless historic process.

Yet an arbitrary construction on our part, in connection with our interest in the relation of the free state to a free society, is responsible for creating these half-truths. We are not Hegelians in constructing our version of the past; history is not the message of God. A variety of interpretations can be right, as we seek actively to judge history. Our original theoretical preoccupation and the search for its solution has manufactured these partial insights cancelling each other out. We have been engaged in trying to understand and to evaluate history. And we are left, in considering the alternative of Marxism as opposed to liberalism, with the romantic conviction about the inevitable indeterminancy in the realm of action. At the end we are basically in the same position as the Enlightenment thinkers when they began the reflections that preceded the French Revolution, which helps account for why an examination of their ideas remains so enduringly alive and such a perennial challenge to social thought.

Index